SELECTED POEMS
of
FRANCIS THOMPSON

---

*Including a Biographical
Note by Wilfrid Meynell*

By

FRANCIS THOMPSON

WITH A CHAPTER FROM
Francis Thompson, Essays, 1917
BY BENJAMIN FRANKLIN FISHER

First published in 1908

British Library Cataloguing-in-Publication Data
A catalogue record for this book is available
from the British Library

CONTENTS

Biographical Sketch of Francis Thompson
by Benjamin Franklin Fisher...........................7

A Biographical Note on Francis Thompson
by Wilfrid Meynell 11

Dedication of "Poems"
Dedication to Wilfrid and Alice Meynell 19

Dedication of "New Poems"
Dedication to Coventry Patmore 21

POEMS ON CHILDREN

DAISY 23

THE POPPY - TO MONICA..........................26

TO MONICA THOUGHT DYING 30

THE MAKING OF VIOLA 33

TO MY GODCHILD - FRANCIS M. W. M............37

'EX ORE INFANTIUM'.............................40

FROM "SISTER SONGS"

A CHILD'S KISS 43

POET AND ANCHORITE 47

THE OMEN 49

THE MIRAGE 51

THE CHILD-WOMAN 53

TO A CHILD HEARD REPEATING
HER MOTHER'S VERSES.........................56

3

A FORETELLING OF THE CHILD'S HUSBAND 59

LOVE IN DIAN'S LAP

BEFORE HER PORTRAIT IN YOUTH 61

TO A POET BREAKING SILENCE. 63

A CARRIER SONG 65

HER PORTRAIT. 68

EPILOGUE - TO THE POET'S SITTER. 74

AFTER HER GOING 76

MISCELLANEOUS POEMS

A FALLEN YEW 79

THE HOUND OF HEAVEN. 83

TO THE DEAD CARDINAL OF WESTMINSTER 89

A DEAD ASTRONOMER - (FATHER PERRY, S.J.) 96

A CORYMBUS FOR AUTUMN. 97

FROM "THE MISTRESS OF VISION" 102

THE AFTER WOMAN 106

LINES - To W.M. 108

THE WAY OF A MAID 109

ODE TO THE SETTING SUN 110

EPILOGUE TO "A JUDGEMENT IN HEAVEN" 120

GRACE OF THE WAY. 122

TO A SNOW-FLAKE 123

ORIENT ODE 124

4

FROM "FROM THE NIGHT OF
FOREBEING" AN ODE AFTER EASTER 131

A COUNSEL OF MODERATION 137

FROM "ASSUMPTA MARIA". 138

FROM "AN ANTHEM OF EARTH" 142

CONTEMPLATION. 148

CORRELATED GREATNESS 151

JULY FUGITIVE. 152

ANY SAINT. 155

FROM "THE VICTORIAN ODE" WRITTEN
FOR THE QUEEN'S GOLDEN JUBILEE DAY, 1897 162

ST MONICA. 165

TO THE SINKING SUN 166

DREAM-TRYST. 168

BUONA NOTTE 169

ARAB LOVE SONG 171

THE KINGDOM OF GOD
"IN NO STRANGE LAND". 172

ENVOY 174

APPRECIATIONS

OF FRANCIS THOMPSON 175

Biographical Sketch
of Francis Thompson

BY BENJAMIN FRANKLIN FISHER

Francis Thompson was born at Preston in Lancashire, England, on the 16th day of December, 1859. His father, Dr. Charles Thompson, was a physician who practised his profession there and later at Ashton-under-lyne.

Very early in life he began to read much poetry; his early reading being mostly from Shakespeare, Scott and Coleridge. Later we find him a constant companion of Milton, Shelley and Shakespeare. In 1870 he was sent to Ushaw, a college near Durham. Here he enjoyed a fortunate freedom—the full opportunity of reading the classics. Even during his college life his extreme sensitiveness, like that of Shelley's youth, made him happiest when alone. He studied for the priesthood but in his nineteenth year being found unfitted, he was advised to give up the idea much to the disappointment of his parents.

Leaving Ushaw he went to Owens College at Manchester to qualify for his father's profession, that of medicine, and although distinguishing himself in Greek and classic work he had no success as a medical student. He says, of this period in his life: "I hated my scientific and medical studies and learned them badly. Now (in after life) even that bad and reluctant knowledge has grown priceless to me. "

While at Manchester he would go to the libraries and to the galleries and museums, thus perhaps unconsciously fitting himself for his after work. Failing in his college examinations on more than one occasion and broken down with a nervous illness, like De Quincey he came addicted to the use of opium. He went to London carrying all his wealth with him, which constisted of two volumes, one in either pocket, *Aeschylus* and *Blake*. However, there he found but little employment, had no money, suffered intensely all the pangs of hunger and dismay, and finally a complete mental and physical wreck, he was for the time being rescued by a Mr. McMaster who took him into his employ in a boot-shop and secured clothes and lodging for him. Francis remained some months with Mr. McMaster and it was at this time that he sent several manuscripts to the magazines. One of these manuscripts was sent to Wilfrid Meynell, editor of *Merry England*.

He left what little employment he had and again became an outcast on the streets of London, where in extreme dispair he was found and befriended by a "girl of the streets" who gave him what aid she might until his later rescue by Wilfrid Meynell.

In the Spring of 1888 Mr. Meynell found Thompson and befriended him; and through his influence and that of his wife, Alice Meynell, Francis was rescued from the streets of London and started on his great literary way which soon brought fame. His *Poems* published in 1893 ran through several editions receiving praise from the reviewers and from Browning; then followed *Sister Songs* in 1895, and *New Poems* in 1897.

He had suffered greatly from bodily disease and melancholy, especially toward the last, and said upon the publication of *New Poems:* "Though my aims are unfulfilled, my place insecure, many things warn me that with this volume, I am probably closing my brief poetic career." His biographer, Everard Meynell, tells us that Thompson never lost confidence in the satisfaction that his poetry was immortal; and this must have been constant inspiration during these troublesome times.

Thompson's early experiences had broken down his health and ten days before his death he was sent to the Hospital of St.

John and St. Elizabeth in London, and there at the age of forty-eight, on November 13, 1907, he passed away at dawn.

Everard Meynell in the closing paragraphs of his admirable *Life of Francis Thompson*, beautifully says: "Suffering alone, he escaped alone, and left none stictly bound on his account. He left his friends to be busy not with his ashes but his works."

A Chapter From
Francis Thompson, Essays, 1917

FRANCIS THOMPSON IN 1894

"I was born in 1858 or 1859 (I never could remember and don't care which) at Preston in Lancashire. Residing there, my mother more than once pointed out to me, as we passed it, the house wherein I was born; and it seemed to me disappointingly like any other house."

A BIOGRAPHICAL NOTE
ON FRANCIS THOMPSON

BY WILFRID MEYNELL

Francis Thompson, a poet of high thinking, "of celestial vision," and of imaginings that found literary images of answering splendour, died in London in the winter of 1907. His life—always a fragile one—doubtless owed its prolongation to "man's unconquerable mind," in him so invincible through all vicissitude that he seemed to add a new significance to Wordsworth's phrase. To his mortal frame was denied the vitality that informs his verse. Howbeit, his verse was himself; he lived every line of it, fulfilling to the last letter his own description of the poet, piteous yet proud:

> He lives detachèd days;
> He serveth not for praise;
>   For gold
>   He is not sold.

> He asketh not world's eyes;
> Nor to world's ears he cries—
>   Saith, "These
>   Shut, if ye please!"

To this aloof moth of a man science was nearly as absorbing an interest as was the mysticism that some thought had eaten him up; and, to give a light example of his actuality, he who had scarce handled a bat since he left Ushaw College, knew every famous score of the last quarter of a century, and left among his papers cricket-verses, trivial yet tragic. One such verse acquaints us incidentally with his Lancashire lineage:

It is little I repair to the matches of the Southron folk,
    Though my own red roses there may blow;
It is little I repair to the matches of the Southron folk,
    Though the red roses crest the caps, I know.
For the field is full of shades as I near the shadowy coast,
And a ghostly batsman plays to the bowling of a ghost,
And I look through my tears on a soundless-clapping host
    As the run-stealers flicker to and fro,
        To and fro.
O my Hornby and my Barlow long ago!

Born at Preston in 1859, the son of a doctor afterwards in practice at Ashton-under-Lyne, he inherited no literary traditions. He had, to be sure, an uncle, an Oxford convert to Catholicism from the ranks of the Anglican clergy, whose name appears on the title page of *Tracts* which, perhaps because for their own Times, seem assuredly for no other. The seven years Francis Thompson passed at Ushaw—a college near Durham, which then possessed few literary traditions besides those of Lingard, Waterton and Wiseman, but can now boast Lafcadio Hearn's as well as Thompson's own—were, no doubt, influential for him; for a certain individualism, still lingering in outstanding seats of learning, gave him a lucky freedom to follow his own bent—the ample reading of the classics. After Ushaw he went to Owens College, to qualify for his father's profession; in his preliminary examination distinguishing himself in Greek.

His attempts to translate dead language into living dated back to these days; though of the list of words, which some who were amused and others who were irritated put down to his own inventing, many were made familiar to him in his intercourse with Milton, with Shelley, with Shakspere—his most vital companions. If these poets went, like Alexander, as far as Chaos, and if Thompson hazarded one step more, as Emerson said Goethe did, Thompson too swung himself safely back again. In Manchester, Literature, if not Melancholy, had already marked him for her own; and it was his *Religio Medici* rather than his *Materia Medica* that he put under his pillow, perhaps the lump of it suggesting to him his after image about the poet's dreaming:

> The hardest pang whereon
> He lays his mutinous head may be a Jacob's stone.

A definite reminiscence of the dissecting-room at Manchester may certainly be discovered in his allusion (in *An Anthem of Earth*) to the heart as

> *Arras'd in purple* like the house of kings,
>   the regal heart that comes at last
>   To stall the grey rat, and the carrion-worm
>   Statelily lodge.

Possibly the sorrow of filial duty unperformed—a sorrow deeper with him than is common among such predestined delinquents—aggravated the bodily ailments which already beset him; and drastic indeed were the remedies he himself prescribed. "Physician, heal thyself": the dire taunt took flesh, as it were, in Francis Thompson, and his plight was visible to all men. Himself he could not save. Biography strangely repeats itself, not in common mental experience only, but also in uncovenanted details of fact and incident. Like De Quincey, whose writings he took into his blood, Thompson had a nervous illness in Manchester; like De Quincey he went to London, and knew Oxford Street for a stony-hearted stepmother; his wealth, like De Quincey's once, lay in two volumes, for he carried Æschylus in

13

one pocket, Blake in the other; and the parallel might, if to profit, be further outdrawn.

To most incongruous modes of making a living he now put his hand. His assistantship in a shop near Leicester Square would have fitted him for the production of a record of *Adventures among Boots*; and later, as a "collector" for a book-seller he must often have bent beneath the sack, which, if heavy, so he might comfort himself, was at least heavy with books. Of these things he spoke with a matter-of-fact, all-accepting, simplicity when, a little later, some verses he sent to a magazine brought him believers, who sought until they found him. After a course of medical treatment, he went to Storrington. That beautiful Sussex village has now its fixed place on the map of English literature. For there it was that Francis Thompson discovered his possibilities as a poet. On its common he met the village child, whom he calls "Daisy," in the verses that are so named. And it was characteristic of this poet that from the ordinary episodes of ordinary days he made his "golden musics." When he saw the sunset at Storrington, the resulting Ode was dotted with local landmarks—the cross, for instance, casting its shadow in the monastery garden. The children of the family in London, into which he was received, were the subjects of *Poppy*, *The Making of Viola*, *To Monica Thought Dying*, *To my Godchild*—all in the first book of *Poems*; while two of their number have a noble heritage in *Sister Songs*. Constant to the end, when he died some newly pencilled lines were found, addressed "To Olivia," a yet younger sister, recalling the strains of fifteen years before:

> I fear to love you, Sweet, because
> Love's the ambassador of loss.

To their mother likewise were addressed the poems of Fair Love, labelled *Love in Dian's Lap*, of which Coventry Patmore said that "Laura might have been proud"; hers also were many of the *New Poems*.

If, therefore, as one critic after another declared, a poet had dropped from the skies—those skies of light—of the Seventeenth Century, he dropped very much upon the spot. "Mr Thompson must simply be Crashaw born again, but born greater," declared the first of his reviewers; and Mr Traill, in *The Nineteenth Century*, inquired: "Where, unless perhaps here and there in a sonnet of Rossetti's, has this sort of sublimated enthusiasm for the bodily and spiritual beauty of womanhood found such expression between the age of the Stuarts and our own?" Mr Traill added boldly his belief—daring then, though acceptable enough now—that "alike in wealth and dignity of imagination, in depth and subtlety of thought and in magic and mastery of language," England possessed in this little volume the evidence of "a new poet of the first rank." More expectedly, Coventry Patmore, in *The Fortnightly Review*, hailed in the new-comer a disciple of their common master, the Florentine Poet of Fair Love, and expressed the opinion that "Mr Thompson's qualities ought to place him in the permanent ranks of fame." The *Hound of Heaven* was to Patmore "one of the very few *great* odes of which the language can boast."

Such pronouncements proved at least that a poet, who had no friend save such as his published poems gained for him, could count on an immediate recognition for high merit. For these tributes, and many more of like welcoming, placed him instantly out of range of the common casualties of criticism. And he had what poets of old to their great sorrow lacked; he had trial by his peers; a kind fate gave him fellow poets among his reviewers.

Perhaps a more convincing sign even than that of professional praise was conveyed by the chance allusion he lighted on later in Lady Burne-Jones's biography of her husband: "The winter's labour," she says, "was cheered by the appearance of a small volume of poems by an author whose name (Francis Thompson) was till then unknown to us. The little book moved him to admiration and hope." And, speaking of *The Hound of Heaven*, Burne-Jones himself said: "Since Gabriel's 'Blessed Damozel' no mystical words have so touched me. Shall I ever forget how I undressed and dressed again, and had to undress again—a thing I most hate—because I could think of nothing else?"

Sister Songs, published in 1895—the poem of which Mr William Archer has said that "Shelley would have adored it"— is a poem to read aloud; for sound and sense herein celebrate their divine nuptials. One of the high memories of the present writer is that of hearing it so read by Mr George Wyndham at the hearthstone of Byron's granddaughter. The lines therein that deal with sex, dormant in the child-girl, yielded the poet perhaps his most amazing imagery. "Superabundance," murmured some— surely a "fault" as happy as was ever son of Adam's. The charge of obscurity brought against the poem was more apt; for who that did not know of his days—and his nights—in the London streets, could follow such a poignant piece of autobiography as this?

> Forlorn, and faint, and stark,
> I had endured through watches of the dark
>   The abashless inquisition of each star;
> Yea, was the outcast mark
>   Of all those heavenly passers' scrutiny;
>   Stood bound and helplessly
> For Time to shoot his barbèd minutes at me;
> Suffered the trampling hoof of every hour
>   In night's slow-wheelèd car;
>   Until the tardy dawn dragged me at length
> From under those dread wheels; and, bled of strength,
>   I waited the inevitable last.
>   Then there came past
> A child; like thee, a spring-flower; but a flower
> Fallen from the budded coronal of Spring,
> And through the city-streets blown withering.
> She passed,—O brave, sad, lovingest, tender thing!—
> And of her own scant pittance did she give,

That I might eat and live:
Then fled, a swift and trackless fugitive.

And how shall that final episode be turned more explicitly? There are still a few things left that cannot be uttered, or, if uttered, that become the counterpart, even for the willing ear, of that "tenuity of the bat's cry" reported to elude the common hearing. It is even as Balzac, great talker himself, says, that everything (especially theology I think) is the cheaper for being discussed. Yet this untold story transcends the mere romance of De Quincey's Ann, and might, indeed, for a moment, reverse Rossetti's just indictment of the life of "Jenny"—"It makes a goblin of the sun." For this "flower fallen from the budded coronal of Spring" took root and flourished, even in London mire, and again the fragrant petals unfolded and the greenery grew.

In *New Poems* Francis Thompson put forth in *The Mistress of Vision* his stark gospel of renunciation . It is the last word of an asceticism which he practised as well as preached—most strait in its abnegation of everything but the beauty his verse, unlike his life, never could renounce. Coventry Patmore, Thompson's true "Captain of Song," used to say that the young poet's prose was even finer than his poetry, and his talk better than both. This was a statement with the true Patmorean touch of paradox. Any way, the talk had no reporter, and of his prose—his "heroic prose," as it has been called—only one example passed, during his life, into book form—the complaint made by Brother Ass, the Body, against its rider, the Soul. This was published under the title of *Health and Holiness*, accompanied by a Note from Father Tyrrell. But his experiences in prose, as a reviewer, were wide as his sympathies, and these were sanely universal. His articles in *The Academy*, under Mr Lewis Hind's editorship, must choke up many a scrapbook. Later, his contributions to *The Athenæum* afforded him his greatest scope and stimulant; and only with his death came the eclipse of his powers. Editors forbore to be angry at his delays, for, after a while of waiting, they got from him, at last, what none else could give at all.

About ten weeks before the darkness fell on him the little flame of his life began visibly to flicker. A change to the country was advised; and he became the carefully tended guest of Mr Wilfrid Blunt—not many miles from the Storrington of his early love, to which, however, not wild arabs could any longer draw him. He was too weak for any travel, save that which brought him back to London—better, he himself said, but surely dying, as it seemed to solicitous eyes.

Ten days before his death he went as a private patient to the Hospital of St John and St Elizabeth, in St John's Wood, and there, at the age of forty-eight, on November 13, 1907, he passed away at dawn—the dawn that was the death-hour in his *Dream Tryst*. He was laid to rest in St Mary's Cemetery, Kensal Green. In his coffin were roses from the garden of Mr George Meredith, inscribed with Mr Meredith's testimony, "A true poet, one of the small band"; and violets from kindred turf went to the dead poet's breast from the hand of her whose praises he had divinely sung. Devoted friends lament him, no less for himself than for his singing. He made all men his debtors, leaving to those who loved him the memory of a unique personality, and to English poetry an imperishable name.

W.M.
The Athenæum,
November 23, 1907.

DEDICATION OF "POEMS"

DEDICATION TO
WILFRID AND ALICE MEYNELL

If the rose in meek duty
  May dedicate humbly
To her grower the beauty
  Wherewith she is comely;
If the mine to the miner
  The jewels that pined in it,
Earth to diviner
  The springs he divined in it;
To the grapes the wine-pitcher
  Their juice that was crushed in it,
Viol to its witcher
  The music lay hushed in it;
If the lips may pay Gladness
  In laughters she wakened,
And the heart to its sadness
  Weeping unslakened,
If the hid and sealed coffer,
  Whose having not his is,
To the loosers may proffer
  Their finding—here this is;
Their lives if all livers
  To the Life of all living,—
To you, O dear givers!
  I give your own giving.

DEDICATION
OF "NEW POEMS"

DEDICATION TO
COVENTRY PATMORE

Lo, my book thinks to look Time's leaguer down,
Under the banner of your spread renown!
Or if these levies of impuissant rhyme
Fall to the overthrow of assaulting Time,
Yet this one page shall fend oblivious shame,
Armed with your crested and prevailing Name.

POEMS ON CHILDREN

DAISY

─────────────

Where the thistle lifts a purple crown
   Six foot out of the turf,
And the harebell shakes on the windy hill—
   O the breath of the distant surf!—

The hills look over on the South,
   And southward dreams the sea;
And, with the sea-breeze hand in hand,
   Came innocence and she.

Where 'mid the gorse the raspberry
   Red for the gatherer springs,
Two children did we stray and talk
   Wise, idle, childish things.

She listened with big-lipped surprise,
   Breast-deep mid flower and spine:
Her skin was like a grape, whose veins
   Run snow instead of wine.

She knew not those sweet words she spake,
   Nor knew her own sweet way;
But there's never a bird, so sweet a song

Thronged in whose throat that day!

Oh, there were flowers in Storrington
    On the turf and on the spray;
But the sweetest flower on Sussex hills
    Was the Daisy-flower that day!

Her beauty smoothed earth's furrowed face!
    She gave me tokens three:—
A look, a word of her winsome mouth,
    And a wild raspberry.

A berry red, a guileless look,
    A still word,—strings of sand!
And yet they made my wild, wild heart
    Fly down to her little hand.

For standing artless as the air,
    And candid as the skies,
She took the berries with her hand,
    And the love with her sweet eyes.

The fairest things have fleetest end:
    Their scent survives their close,
But the rose's scent is bitterness
    To him that loved the rose!

She looked a little wistfully,
    Then went her sunshine way:—
The sea's eye had a mist on it,
    And the leaves fell from the day.

She went her unremembering way,
    She went and left in me
The pang of all the partings gone,

And partings yet to be.

She left me marvelling why my soul
   Was sad that she was glad;
At all the sadness in the sweet,
   The sweetness in the sad.

Still, still I seemed to see her, still
   Look up with soft replies,
And take the berries with her hand,
   And the love with her lovely eyes.

Nothing begins, and nothing ends,
   That is not paid with moan;
For we are born in other's pain,
   And perish in our own.

THE POPPY

TO MONICA

Summer set lip to earth's bosom bare.
And left the flushed print in a poppy there:
Like a yawn of fire from the grass it came,
And the fanning wind puffed it to flapping flame.

With burnt mouth red like a lion's it drank
The blood of the sun as he slaughtered sank,
And dipped its cup in the purpurate shine
When the eastern conduits ran with wine.

Till it grew lethargied with fierce bliss,
And hot as a swinked gipsy is,
And drowsed in sleepy savageries,
With mouth wide a-pout for a sultry kiss.

A child and man paced side by side,
Treading the skirts of eventide;
But between the clasp of his hand and hers
Lay, felt not, twenty withered years.

She turned, with the rout of her dusk South hair,
And saw the sleeping gipsy there;
And snatched and snapped it in swift child's whim,
With—"Keep it, long as you live!"—to him.

And his smile, as nymphs from their laving meres,

Trembled up from a bath of tears;
And joy, like a mew sea-rocked apart,
Tossed on the wave of his troubled heart.

For *he* saw what she did not see,
That—as kindled by its own fervency—
The verge shrivelled inward smoulderingly:

And suddenly 'twixt his hand and hers
He knew the twenty withered years—
No flower, but twenty shrivelled years.

"Was never such thing until this hour,"
Low to his heart he said; "the flower
Of sleep brings wakening to me,
And of oblivion memory."

"Was never this thing to me," he said,
"Though with bruisèd poppies my feet are red!"
And again to his own heart very low:
"O child!I love, for I love and know;

"But you, who love nor know at all
The diverse chambers in Love's guest-hall,
Where some rise early, few sit long:
In how differing accents hear the throng
His great Pentecostal tongue;

"Who know not love from amity,
Nor my reported self from me;
A fair fit gift is this, meseems,
You give—this withering flower of dreams.

"O frankly fickle, and fickly true,
Do you know what the days will do to you?

To your Love and you what the days will do,
O frankly fickle, and fickly true?

"You have loved me, Fair, three lives—or days:
'Twill pass with the passing of my face.
But where *I* go, your face goes too,
To watch lest I play false to you.

"I am but, my sweet, your foster-lover,
Knowing well when certain years are over
You vanish from me to another;
Yet I know, and love, like the foster-mother.

"So, frankly fickle, and fickly true!
For my brief life—while I take from you
This token, fair and fit, meseems,
For me—this withering flower of dreams."

* * * * * * *

The sleep-flower sways in the wheat its head,
Heavy with dreams, as that with bread:
The goodly grain and the sun-flushed sleeper
The reaper reaps, and Time the reaper.

I hang 'mid men my needless head,
And my fruit is dreams, as theirs is bread:
The goodly men and the sun-hazed sleeper
Time shall reap, but after the reaper
The world shall glean of me, me the sleeper!

Love! love! your flower of withered dream
In leavèd rhyme lies safe, I deem,
Sheltered and shut in a nook of rhyme,
From the reaper man, and his reaper Time.

28

Love! *I* fall into the claws of Time:
But lasts within a leavèd rhyme
All that the world of me esteems—
My withered dreams, my withered dreams.

TO MONICA
THOUGHT DYING

———————————

You, O the piteous you!
Who all the long night through
Anticipatedly
Disclose yourself to me
Already in the ways
Beyond our human comfortable days;
    How can you deem what Death
    Impitiably saith
    To me, who listening wake
    For your poor sake?
    When a grown woman dies
You know we think unceasingly
What things she said, how sweet, how wise;
And these do make our misery.
    But you were (you to me
The dead anticipatedly!)
You—eleven years, was't not, or so?—
    Were just a child, you know;
    And so you never said
Things sweet immeditatably and wise
To interdict from closure my wet eyes:
    But foolish things, my dead, my dead!
    Little and laughable,
    Your age that fitted well.
And was it such things all unmemorable,
    Was it such things could make
Me sob all night for your implacable sake?

Yet, as you said to me,
In pretty make-believe of revelry,
So the night long said Death
With his magniloquent breath;
(And that remembered laughter
Which in our daily uses followed after,
Was all untuned to pity and to awe):
"A cup of chocolate,
One farthing is the rate,
You drink it through a straw."

How could I know, how know
Those laughing words when drenched with sobbing so?
Another voice than yours, than yours, he hath!
My dear, was't worth his breath,
His mighty utterance?—yet he saith, and saith!
This dreadful Death to his own dreadfulness
Doth dreadful wrong,
This dreadful childish babble on his tongue!
That iron tongue made to speak sentences,
And wisdom insupportably complete,
Why should it only say the long night through,
In mimicry of you,—
"A cup of chocolate,
One farthing is the rate,
You drink it through a straw, a straw, a straw!"
Oh, of all sentences,
Piercingly incomplete!
Why did you teach that fatal mouth to draw,
Child, impermissible awe,
From your old trivialness?
Why have you done me this
Most unsustainable wrong,
And into Death's control

31

Betrayed the secret places of my soul?
    Teaching him that his lips,
Uttering their native earthquake and eclipse,
    Could never so avail
To rend from hem to hem the ultimate veil
    Of this most desolate
Spirit, and leave it stripped and desecrate,—
    Nay, never so have wrung
From eyes and speech weakness unmanned, unmeet;
As when his terrible dotage to repeat
Its little lesson learneth at your feet;
    As when he sits among
    His sepulchres, to play
With broken toys your hand has cast away,
With derelict trinkets of the darling young.
Why have you taught—that he might so complete
    His awful panoply
    From your cast playthings—why,
This dreadful childish babble to his tongue,
    Dreadful and sweet?

THE MAKING OF VIOLA

I

The Father of Heaven.
 Spin, daughter Mary, spin,
 Twirl your wheel with silver din;
 Spin, daughter Mary, spin,
  Spin a tress for Viola.
Angels.
 Spin, Queen Mary, a
 Brown tress for Viola!

II

The Father of Heaven.
 Weave, hands angelical,
 Weave a woof of flesh to pall—
 Weave, hands angelical—
  Flesh to pall our Viola.
Angels.
 Weave, singing brothers, a
 Velvet flesh for Viola!

III

The Father of Heaven.
 Scoop, young Jesus, for her eyes,
 Wood-browned pools of Paradise—
 Young Jesus, for the eyes,
  For the eyes of Viola.

Angels.
>Tint, Prince Jesus, a
>Duskèd eye for Viola!

IV

The Father of Heaven.
>Cast a star therein to drown,
>Like a torch in cavern brown,
>Sink a burning star to drown
>>Whelmed in eyes of Viola.

Angels.
>Lave, Prince Jesus, a
>Star in eyes of Viola!

V

The Father of Heaven.
>Breathe, Lord Paraclete,
>To a bubbled crystal meet—
>Breathe, Lord Paraclete—
>>Crystal soul for Viola.

Angels.
>Breathe, Regal Spirit, a
>Flashing soul for Viola!

VI

The Father of Heaven.
>Child-angels, from your wings
>Fall the roseal hoverings,
>Child-angels, from your wings,
>>On the cheeks of Viola.

Angels.
>Linger, rosy reflex, a

Quenchless stain, on Viola!

All things being accomplished, saith the Father of Heaven.

Bear her down, and bearing, sing,
Bear her down on spyless wing,
Bear her down, and bearing, sing,
      With a sound of viola.
Angels.
Music as her name is, a
Sweet sound of Viola!

VIII

Wheeling angels, past espial,
Danced her down with sound of viol;
Wheeling angels, past espial,
      Descanting on "Viola."
Angels.
Sing, in our footing, a
Lovely lilt of "Viola!"

IX

Baby smiled, mother wailed,
Earthward while the sweetling sailed;
Mother smiled, baby wailed,
      When to earth came Viola.
And her elders shall say:—
So soon have we taught you a
Way to weep, poor Viola!

X

Smile, sweet baby, smile,

For you will have weeping-while;
Native in your Heaven is smile,—
    But your weeping, Viola?

Whence your smiles we know, but ah?
Whence your weeping, Viola?—
Our first gift to you is a
Gift of tears, my Viola!

TO MY GODCHILD

FRANCIS M. W. M.

This labouring, vast, Tellurian galleon,
Riding at anchor off the orient sun,
Had broken its cable, and stood out to space
Down some frore Arctic of the aërial ways:
And now, back warping from the inclement main,
Its vaporous shroudage drenched with icy rain,
It swung into its azure roads again;
When, floated on the prosperous sun-gale, you
Lit, a white halcyon auspice, 'mid our frozen crew.

To the Sun, stranger, surely you belong,
Giver of golden days and golden song;
Nor is it by an all-unhappy plan
You bear the name of me, his constant Magian.
Yet ah! from any other that it came,
Lest fated to my fate you be, as to my name.
When at the first those tidings did they bring,
My heart turned troubled at the ominous thing:
Though well may such a title him endower,
For whom a poet's prayer implores a poet's power.
The Assisian, who kept plighted faith to three,
To Song, to Sanctitude, and Poverty,

(In two alone of whom most singers prove
A fatal faithfulness of during love!);
He the sweet Sales, of whom we scarcely ken

How God he could love more, he so loved men;
The crown and crowned of Laura and Italy;
And Fletcher's fellow—from these, and not from me,
Take you your name, and take your legacy!

Or, if a right successive you declare
When worms, for ivies, intertwine my hair,
Take but this Poesy that now followeth
My clayey hest with sullen servile breath,
Made then your happy freedman by testating death.
My song I do but hold for you in trust,
I ask you but to blossom from my dust.
When you have compassed all weak I began,
Diviner poet, and ah! diviner man;
The man at feud with the perduring child
In you before song's altar nobly reconciled;
From the wise heavens I half shall smile to see
How little a world, which owned you, needed me.
If, while you keep the vigils of the night,
For your wild tears make darkness all too bright,
Some lone orb through your lonely window peeps,
As it played lover over your sweet sleeps;
Think it a golden crevice in the sky,
Which I have pierced but to behold you by!

And when, immortal mortal, droops your head,
And you, the child of deathless song, are dead;
Then, as you search with unaccustomed glance
The ranks of Paradise for my countenance,
Turn not your tread along the Uranian sod
Among the bearded counsellors of God;
For if in Eden as on earth are we,
I sure shall keep a younger company:
Pass where beneath their rangèd gonfalons
The starry cohorts shake their shielded suns,

The dreadful mass of their enridgèd spears;
Pass where majestical the eternal peers, ·
The stately choice of the great Saintdom, meet—
A silvern segregation, globed complete
In sandalled shadow of the Triune feet;
Pass by where wait, young poet-wayfarer,
Your cousined clusters, emulous to share
With you the roseal lightnings burning 'mid their hair;
Pass the crystalline sea, the Lampads seven:—
Look for me in the nurseries of Heaven.

'EX ORE INFANTIUM'

Little Jesus, wast Thou shy
Once, and just so small as I?
And what did it feel like to be
Out of Heaven, and just like me?
Didst Thou sometimes think of*there*,
And ask where all the angels were?
I should think that I would cry
For my house all made of sky;
I would look about the air,
And wonder where my angels were;
And at waking 'twould distress me—
Not an angel there to dress me!
Hadst Thou ever any toys,
Like us little girls and boys?
And didst Thou play in Heaven with all
The angels that were not too tall,
With stars for marbles?Did the things
Play*Can you see me?* through their wings?
And did Thy Mother let Thee spoil
Thy robes, with playing on*our*soil?
How nice to have them always new
In Heaven, because 'twas quite clean blue!

Didst Thou kneel at night to pray,
And didst Thou join Thy hands, this way?
And did they tire sometimes, being young,
And make the prayer seem very long?
And dost Thou like it best, that we
Should join our hands to pray to Thee?

I used to think, before I knew,
The prayer not said unless we do.
And did Thy Mother at the night
Kiss Thee, and fold the clothes in right?
And didst Thou feel quite good in bed,
Kissed, and sweet, and thy prayers said?

Thou canst not have forgotten all
That it feels like to be small:
And Thou know'st I cannot pray
To Thee in my father's way—
When Thou wast so little, say,
Couldst Thou talk Thy Father's way?—
So, a little Child, come down
And hear a child's tongue like Thy own;
Take me by the hand and walk,
And listen to my baby-talk.
To Thy Father show my prayer
(He will look, Thou art so fair),
And say: 'O Father, I, Thy Son,
Bring the prayer of a little one.'

And He will smile, that children's tongue
Has not changed since Thou wast young!

FROM
"SISTER SONGS"

A CHILD'S KISS

Where its umbrage[1] was enrooted,
    Sat white-suited,
Sat green-amiced, and bare-footed,
    Spring amid her minstrelsy;
There she sat amid her ladies,
    Where the shade is
Sheen as Enna mead ere Hades'
    Gloom fell thwart Persephone.
Dewy buds were interstrown
Through her tresses hanging down,
    And her feet
    Were most sweet,
Tinged like sea-stars, rosied brown.
A throng of children like to flowers were sown
About the grass beside, or clomb her knee:
I looked who were that favoured company.
    And one there stood
    Against the beamy flood
Of sinking day, which, pouring its abundance,
Sublimed the illuminous and volute redundance
Of locks that, half dissolving, floated round her face;
    As see I might

Far off a lily-cluster poised in sun
    Dispread its gracile curls of light
I knew what chosen child was there in place!
I knew there might no brows be, save of one,
    With such Hesperian fulgence compassèd,
Which in her moving seemed to wheel about her head.

O Spring's little children, more loud your lauds upraise,
For this is even Sylvia, with her sweet, feat ways!
    Your lovesome labours lay away,
    And prank you out in holiday,
      For syllabling to Sylvia;
And all you birds on branches, lave your mouths with May,
    To bear with me this burthen
      For singing to Sylvia!

Spring, goddess, is it thou, desirèd long?
And art thou girded round with this young train?—
If ever I did do thee ease in song,
Now of thy grace let me one meed obtain,
      And list thou to one plain.
      Oh, keep still in thy train
After the years when others therefrom fade,
      This tiny, well-belovèd maid!
To whom the gate of my heart's fortalice,
      With all which in it is,
And the shy self who doth therein immew him
'Gainst what loud leaguers battailously woo him,
      I, bribèd traitor to him,
      Set open for one kiss.

    A kiss? for a child's kiss?
    Aye, goddess, even for this.
Once, bright Sylviola! in days not far,
Once—in that nightmare-time which still doth haunt

My dreams, a grim, unbidden visitant—
   Forlorn, and faint, and stark,
I had endured through watches of the dark
  The abashless inquisition of each star,
Yea, was the outcast mark
     Of all those heavenly passers' scrutiny;
     Stood bound and helplessly
For Time to shoot his barbèd minutes at me;
Suffered the trampling hoof of every hour
    In night's slow-wheelèd car;
  Until the tardy dawn dragged me at length
  From under those dread wheels; and, bled of strength,
    I waited the inevitable last.
      Then there came past
A child; like thee, a spring-flower; but a flower
Fallen from the budded coronal of Spring,
And through the city-streets blown withering.
She passed,—O brave, sad, lovingest, tender thing!—
And of her own scant pittance did she give,
    That I might eat and live:
Then fled, a swift and trackless fugitive.
    Therefore I kissed in thee
The heart of Childhood, so divine for me;
     And her, through what sore ways,
     And what unchildish days,
Borne from me now, as then, a trackless fugitive.
    Therefore I kissed in thee
    Her, child! and innocency,
And spring, and all things that have gone from me,
    And that shall never be;
All vanished hopes, and all most hopeless bliss,
    Came with thee to my kiss.
And ah! so long myself had strayed afar
From child, and woman, and the boon earth's green,
And all wherewith life's face is fair beseen;

Journeying its journey bare
Five suns, except of the all-kissing sun
    Unkissed of one;
    Almost I had forgot
    The healing harms,
And whitest witchery, a-lurk in that
Authentic cestus of two girdling arms:
    And I remembered not
  The subtle sanctities which dart
From childish lips' unvalued precious brush,
Nor how it makes the sudden lilies push
  Between the loosening fibres of the heart.
    Then, that thy little kiss
    Should be to me all this,
Let workaday wisdom blink sage lids thereat;
Which towers a flight three hedgerows high, poor bat!
  And straightway charts me out the empyreal air.
Its chart I wing not by, its canon of worth
Scorn not, nor reck though mine should breed it mirth:
And howso thou and I may be disjoint,
Yet still my falcon spirit makes her point
    Over the covert where
Thou, sweetest quarry, hast put in from her!

Soul, hush these sad numbers, too sad to upraise
In hymning bright Sylvia, unlearn'd in such ways!
  Our mournful moods lay we away,
  And prank our thoughts in holiday,
    For syllabling to Sylvia;
When all the birds on branches lave their mouths with May,
  To bear with us this burthen,
    For singing to Sylvia!

POET AND ANCHORITE

———————————

Love and love's beauty only hold their revels
In life's familiar, penetrable levels:
    What of its ocean-floor?
    I dwell there evermore.
    From almost earliest youth
    I raised the lids o' the truth,
And forced her bend on me her shrinking sight;
Ever I knew me Beauty's eremite,
  In antre of this lowly body set.
    Girt with a thirsty solitude of soul.
     Nathless I not forget
How I have, even as the anchorite,
  I too, imperishing essences that console.
Under my ruined passions, fallen and sere,
  The wild dreams stir like little radiant girls,
Whom in the moulted plumage of the year
  Their comrades sweet have buried to the curls.
Yet, though their dedicated amorist,
How often do I bid my visions hist,
  Deaf to them, pleading all their piteous fills;
Who weep, as weep the maidens of the mist
  Clinging the necks of the unheeding hills:
And their tears wash them lovelier than before,
That from grief's self our sad delight grows more,
Fair are the soul's uncrispèd calms, indeed,
  Endiapered with many a spiritual form
    Of blosmy-tinctured weed;
But scarce itself is conscious of the store
  Suckled by it, and only after storm

47

Casts up its loosened thoughts upon the shore.
    To this end my deeps are stirred;
   And I deem well why life unshared
   Was ordainèd me of yore.
   In pairing-time, we know, the bird
   Kindles to its deepmost splendour,
      And the tender
    Voice is tenderest in its throat;
Were its love, for ever nigh it,
      Never by it,
    It might keep a vernal note,
The crocean and amethystine
     In their pristine
    Lustre linger on its coat.
Therefore must my song-bower lone be,
     That my tone be
   Fresh with dewy pain alway;
She, who scorns my dearest care ta'en,
     An uncertain
   Shadow of the sprite of May.

THE OMEN

Yet is there more, whereat none guesseth, love!
  Upon the ending of my deadly night
(Whereof thou hast not the surmise, and slight
Is all that any mortal knows thereof),
  Thou wert to me that earnest of day's light,
When, like the back of a gold-mailèd saurian
  Heaving its slow length from Nilotic slime,
The first long gleaming fissure runs Aurorian
  Athwart the yet dun firmament of prime.
Stretched on the margin of the cruel sea
  Whence they had rescued me,
With faint and painful pulses was I lying;
    Not yet discerning well
If I had 'scaped, or were an icicle,
    Whose thawing is its dying.
Like one who sweats before a despot's gate,
Summoned by some presaging scroll of fate,
And knows not whether kiss or dagger wait;
And all so sickened is his countenance,
The courtiers buzz, "Lo, doomed!"
and look at him askance:—
    At Fate's dread portal then
    Even so stood I, I ken,
Even so stood I, between a joy and fear,
And said to mine own heart, "Now if the end be here!"

    They say, Earth's beauty seems completest
      To them that on their death-beds rest;
    Gentle lady! she smiles sweetest

Just ere she clasp us to her breast.
And I,—now *my* Earth's countenance grew bright,
Did she but smile me towards that nuptial-night?
But whileas on such dubious bed I lay,
   One unforgotten day,
  As a sick child waking sees
   Wide-eyed daisies
 Gazing on it from its hand,
 Slipped there for its dear amazes;
 So between thy father's knees
   I saw *thee* stand,
   And through my hazes
Of pain and fear thine eyes' young wonder shone.
Then, as flies scatter from a carrion,
 Or rooks in spreading gyres like broken smoke
 Wheel, when some sound their quietude has broke,
Fled, at thy countenance, all that doubting spawn:
   The heart which I had questioned spoke,
A cry impetuous from its depths was drawn,—
"I take the omen of this face of dawn!"
And with the omen to my heart cam'st thou.
   Even with a spray of tears
That one light draft was fixed there for the years.
   And now?—
The hours I tread ooze memories of thee, Sweet!
  Beneath my casual feet.
  With rainfall as the lea,
  The day is drenched with thee;
 In little exquisite surprises
Bubbling deliciousness of thee arises
   From sudden places,
  Under the common traces
Of my most lethargied and customed paces.

THE MIRAGE

As an Arab journeyeth
Through a sand of Ayaman,
Lean Thirst, lolling its cracked tongue,
Lagging by his side along;
And a rusty-wingèd Death
Grating its low flight before,
Casting ribbèd shadows o'er
The blank desert, blank and tan:
He lifts by hap toward where the morning's roots are
            His weary stare,—
        Sees, although they plashless mutes are,
            Set in a silver air
Fountains of gelid shoots are,
        Making the daylight fairest fair;
    Sees the palm and tamarind

Tangle the tresses of a phantom wind;—
A sight like innocence when one has sinned!
A green and maiden freshness smiling there,
        While with unblinking glare
The tawny-hided desert crouches watching her.

        'Tis a vision:
    Yet the greeneries Elysian
    He has known in tracts afar;
    Thus the enamouring fountains flow,
    Those the very palms that grow,
By rare-gummed Sava, or Herbalimar.—

Such a watered dream has tarried
Trembling on my desert arid;
   Even so
Its lovely gleamings
   Seemings show
Of things not seemings;
   And I gaze,
Knowing that, beyond my ways,
   Verily
   All these *are*, for these are she.
Eve no gentlier lays her cooling cheek
On the burning brow of the sick earth,
   Sick with death, and sick with birth,
Aeon to aeon, in secular fever twirled,
   Than thy shadow soothes this weak
   And distempered being of mine.
In all I work, my hand includeth thine;
   Thou rushest down in every stream
Whose passion frets my spirit's deepening gorge;
Unhood'st mine eyas-heart, and fliest my dream;
   Thou swing'st the hammers of my forge;
As the innocent moon, that nothing does but shine,
Moves all the labouring surges of the world.
   Pierce where thou wilt the springing thought in me,
And there thy pictured countenance lies enfurled,
   As in the cut fern lies the imaged tree.
   This poor song that sings of thee,
   This fragile song, is but a curled
   Shell outgathered from thy sea,
   And murmurous still of its nativity.

THE CHILD-WOMAN

O thou most dear!
Who art thy sex's complex harmony
    God-set more facilely;
    To thee may love draw near
    Without one blame or fear,
Unchidden save by his humility:
Thou Perseus' Shield! wherein I view secure
The mirrored Woman's fateful-fair allure!
Whom Heaven still leaves a twofold dignity,
As girlhood gentle, and as boyhood free;
With whom no most diaphanous webs enwind
The barèd limbs of the rebukeless mind.
Wild Dryad! all unconscious of thy tree,
    With which indissolubly
The tyrannous time shall one day make thee whole;
Whose frank arms pass unfretted through its bole:
    Who wear'st thy femineity
Light as entrailèd blossoms, that shalt find
It erelong silver shackles unto thee.
Thou whose young sex is yet but in thy soul;—
    As hoarded in the vine
Hang the gold skins of undelirious wine,
As air sleeps, till it toss its limbs in breeze:—
  In whom the mystery which lures and sunders,
    Grapples and thrusts apart; endears, estranges;
  —The dragon to its own Hesperides—
  Is gated under slow-revolving changes,
Manifold doors of heavy-hingèd years.
  So once, ere Heaven's eyes were filled with wonders

To see Laughter rise from Tears,
Lay in beauty not yet mighty,
Conchèd in translucencies,
The antenatal Aphrodite,
Caved magically under magic seas;
Caved dreamlessly beneath the dreamful seas.

"Whose sex is in thy soul!"
What think we of thy soul?
Which has no parts, and cannot grow,
Unfurled not from an embryo;
Born of full stature, lineal to control;
And yet a pigmy's yoke must undergo.
Yet must keep pace and tarry, patient, kind,
With its unwilling scholar, the dull, tardy mind;
Must be obsequious to the body's powers,
Whose low hands mete its paths,
set ope and close its ways;
Must do obeisance to the days,
And wait the little pleasure of the hours;
Yea, ripe for kingship, yet must be
Captive in statuted minority!
So is all power fulfilled, as soul in thee.
So still the ruler by the ruled takes rule,
And wisdom weaves itself i' the loom o' the fool.
The splendent sun no splendour can display,
Till on gross things he dash his broken ray,
From cloud and tree and flower re-tossed in prismy spray.
Did not obstruction's vessel hem it in,
Force were not force, would spill itself in vain
We know the Titan by his champèd chain.
Stay is heat's cradle, it is rocked therein,
And by check's hand is burnished into light;
If hate were none, would love burn lowlier bright?
God's Fair were guessed scarce but for opposite sin;

Yea, and His Mercy, I do think it well,
Is flashed back from the brazen gates of Hell.
     The heavens decree
All power fulfil itself as soul in thee.
For supreme Spirit subject was to clay,
  And Law from its own servants learned a law,
And Light besought a lamp unto its way,
     And Awe was reined in awe,
   At one small house of Nazareth;
    And Golgotha
Saw Breath to breathlessness resign its breath,
And Life do homage for its crown to death.

TO A CHILD HEARD
REPEATING HER MOTHER'S VERSES

As a nymph's carven head sweet water drips,
For others oozing so the cool delight
Which cannot steep her stiffened mouth of stone—
Thy nescient lips repeat maternal strains.
        Memnonian lips!
Smitten with singing from thy mother's east,
    And murmurous with music not their own:
    Nay, the lips flexile, while the mind alone
            A passionless statue stands.
            Oh, pardon, innocent one!
    Pardon at thine unconscious hands!
"Murmurous with music not their own," I say?
And in that saying how do I missay,
            When from the common sands
Of poorest common speech of common day
Thine accents sift the golden musics out!
        And ah, we poets, I misdoubt,
        Are little more than thou!
We speak a lesson taught we know not how,
        And what it is that from us flows
The hearer better than the utterer knows.

* * * * *

And thou, bright girl, not long shalt thou repeat
Idly the music from thy mother caught;
        Not vainly has she wrought,

56

Not vainly from the cloudward-jetting turret
Of her aërial mind, for thy weak feet,
Let down the silken ladder of her thought.
　　She bare thee with a double pain,
　　　　Of the body and the spirit;
　　Thou thy fleshly weeds hast ta'en,
　　　　Thy diviner weeds inherit!
The precious streams which through thy young lips roll
Shall leave their lovely delta in thy soul:
　　Where sprites of so essential kind
　　　　Set their paces,
　　Surely they shall leave behind
　　　　The green traces
　　Of their sportance in the mind,
And thou shalt, ere we well may know it,
　　Turn that daintiness, a poet,—
　　　　Elfin-ring
　　Where sweet fancies foot and sing.

　　So it may be, so it *shall* be,—
　　Oh, take the prophecy from me!
What if the old fastidious sculptor, Time,
　　This crescent marvel of his hands
　　Carveth all too painfully,
And I who prophesy shall never see?
What if the niche of its predestined rhyme,
　Its aching niche, too long expectant stands?
　　Yet shall he after sore delays
　　On some exultant day of days
　　The white enshrouding childhood raise
From thy fair spirit, finished for our gaze;
　　While we (but 'mongst that happy "we"
　　　　The prophet cannot be!)
While we behold with no astonishments,
With that serene fulfilment of delight

Wherewith we view the sight
When the stars pitch the golden tents
Of their high campment on the plains of night.
Why should amazement be our satellite?
What wonder in such things?
If angels have hereditary wings,
If not by Salic law is handed down
The poet's crown,
To thee, born in the purple of the throne,
The laurel must belong:
Thou, in thy mother's right
Descendant of Castalian-chrismed kings—
O Princess of the Blood of Song!

A FORETELLING OF
THE CHILD'S HUSBAND

But on a day whereof I think,
One shall dip his hand to drink
In that still water of thy soul,
And its imaged tremors race
Over thy joy-troubled face,
As the intervolved reflections roll
From a shaken fountain's brink,
With swift light wrinkling its alcove.
From the hovering wing of Love
The warm stain shall flit roseal on thy cheek,
Then, sweet blushet! whenas he,
The destined paramount of thy universe,
Who has no worlds to sigh for, ruling thee,
Àscends his vermeil throne of empery,
One grace alone I seek.
Oh! may this treasure-galleon of my verse,
Fraught with its golden passion, oared with cadent rhyme,
Set with a towering press of fantasies,
Drop safely down the time,
Leaving mine islèd self behind it far
Soon to be sunken in the abysm of seas,
(As down the years the splendour voyages
From some long ruined and night-submergèd star),
And in thy subject sovereign's havening heart
Anchor the freightage of its virgin ore;
Adding its wasteful more
To his own overflowing treasury.

So through his river mine shall reach thy sea,
    Bearing its confluent part;
    In his pulse mine shall thrill;
 And the quick heart shall quicken
    from the heart that's still.

Now pass your ways, fair bird, and pass your ways,
    If you will;
    I have you through the days!
    A flit or hold you still,
    And perch you where you list
      On what wrist,—
    You are mine through the times!
I have caught you fast for ever in a tangle of sweet rhymes.
    And in your young maiden morn,
      You may scorn,
      But you must be
    Bound and sociate to me;
 With this thread from out the tomb my
    dead hand shall tether thee!

LOVE IN DIAN'S LAP

BEFORE HER
PORTRAIT IN YOUTH

———————————

As lovers, banished from their lady's face
  And hopeless of her grace,
Fashion a ghostly sweetness in its place,
  Fondly adore
Some stealth-won cast attire she wore,
  A kerchief or a glove:
  And at the lover's beck
 Into the glove there fleets the hand,
 Or at impetuous command
Up from the kerchief floats the virgin neck:
So I, in very lowlihead of love,—
  Too shyly reverencing
 To let one thought's light footfall smooth
Tread near the living, consecrated thing,—
  Treasure me thy cast youth.
This outworn vesture, tenantless of thee,
  Hath yet my knee,
 For that, with show and semblance fair
  Of the past Her
Who once the beautiful, discarded raiment bare,
  It cheateth me.

As gale to gale drifts breath
    Of blossoms' death,
So dropping down the years from hour to hour
    This dead youth's scent is wafted me to-day:
I sit, and from the fragrance dream the flower.
        So, then, she looked (I say);
        And so her front sunk down
Heavy beneath the poet's iron crown:
        On her mouth museful sweet—
        (Even as the twin lips meet)
        Did thought and sadness greet:
            Sighs
        In those mournful eyes
    So put on visibilities;
As viewless ether turns, in deep on deep, to dyes.
        Thus, long ago,
She kept her meditative paces slow
Through maiden meads, with wavèd shadow and gleam
Of locks half-lifted on the winds of dream,
Till love up-caught her to his chariot's glow.
Yet, voluntary, happier Proserpine!
    This drooping flower of youth thou lettest fall
    I, faring in the cockshut-light, astray,
        Find on my 'lated way,
    And stoop, and gather for memorial,
And lay it on my bosom, and make it mine.
To this, the all of love the stars allow me,
        I dedicate and vow me.
        I reach back through the days
A trothed hand to the dead the last trump shall not raise.
        The water-wraith that cries
From those eternal sorrows of thy pictured eyes
Entwines and draws me down their soundless intricacies!

TO A POET BREAKING SILENCE

Too wearily had we and song
Been left to look and left to long,
Yea, song and we to long and look,
Since thine acquainted feet forsook
The mountain where the Muses hymn
For Sinai and the Seraphim.
Now in both the mountains' shine
Dress thy countenance, twice divine!
From Moses and the Muses draw
The Tables of thy double Law!
His rod-born fount and Castaly
Let the one rock bring forth for thee,
Renewing so from either spring
The songs which both thy countries sing:
Or we shall fear lest, heavened thus long,
Thou should'st forget thy native song,
And mar thy mortal melodies
With broken stammer of the skies.

Ah! let the sweet birds of the Lord
With earth's waters make accord;
Teach how the crucifix may be
Carven from the laurel-tree,
Fruit of the Hesperides
Burnish take on Eden-trees,
The Muses' sacred grove be wet
With the red dew of Olivet,
And Sappho lay her burning brows
In white Cecilia's lap of snows!

* * * * *

I think thy girlhood's watchers must
Have took thy folded songs on trust,
And felt them, as one feels the stir
Of still lightnings in the hair,
When conscious hush expects the cloud
To speak the golden secret loud
Which tacit air is privy to;
Flasked in the grape the wine they knew,
Ere thy poet-mouth was able
For its first young starry babble.
Keep'st thou not yet that subtle grace?
Yea, in this silent interspace,
God sets His poems in thy face!

The loom which mortal verse affords,
Out of weak and mortal words,
Wovest thou thy singing-weed in,
To a rune of thy far Eden.
Vain are all disguises!Ah,
Heavenly *incognita*!
Thy mien bewrayeth through that wrong
The great Uranian House of Song!
As the vintages of earth
Taste of the sun that riped their birth,
We know what never cadent Sun
Thy lampèd clusters throbbed upon,
What plumed feet the winepress trod;
Thy wine is flavorous of God.
Whatever singing-robe thou wear
Has the Paradisal air;
And some gold feather it has kept
Shows what Floor it lately swept!

A CARRIER SONG

Since you have waned from us,
  Fairest of women!
I am a darkened cage
  Song cannot hymn in.
My songs have followed you,
  Like birds the summer;
Ah! bring them back to me,
  Swiftly, dear comer!
      Seraphim,
      Her to hymn,
      Might leave their portals;
      And at my feet learn
      The harping of mortals!

Whereso your angel is,
  My angel goeth;
I am left guardianless,
  Paradise knoweth!
I have no Heaven left
  To weep my wrongs to;
Heaven, when you went from us,
  Went with my songs too.
      Seraphim,
      Her to hymn,
      Might leave their portals;
      And at my feet learn
      The harping of mortals!

I have no angels left
　　Now, Sweet, to pray to:
Where you have made your shrine
　　They are away to.
They have struck Heaven's tent,
　　And gone to cover you:
Whereso you keep your state
　　Heaven is pitched over you!
　　　　Seraphim,
　　　　Her to hymn,
　　　　Might leave their portals;
　　　　And at my feet learn
　　　　The harping of mortals!

She that is Heaven's Queen
　　Her title borrows,
For that she pitiful
　　Beareth our sorrows.
So thou, *Regina mî,*
　　Spes infirmorum;
With all our grieving crowned
　　Mater dolorum!
　　　　Seraphim,
　　　　Her to hymn,
　　　　Might leave their portals;
　　　　And at my feet learn
　　　　The harping of mortals!

Yet, envious coveter
　　Of other's grieving!
This lonely longing yet
　　'Scapeth your reaving.
Cruel! to take from a
　　Sinner his Heaven!
Think you with contrite smiles

To be forgiven?
    Seraphim,
    Her to hymn,
    Might leave their portals;
    And at my feet learn
    The harping of mortals!

Penitent! give me back
  Angels, and Heaven;
Render your stolen self,
  And be forgiven!
How frontier Heaven from you?
  For my soul prays, Sweet,
Still to your face in Heaven,
  Heaven in your face, Sweet!
    Seraphim,
    Her to hymn,
    Might leave their portals;
    And at my feet learn
    The harping of mortals!

HER PORTRAIT

Oh, but the heavenly grammar did I hold
Of that high speech which angels' tongues turn gold!
So should her deathless beauty take no wrong,
Praised in her own great kindred's fit and cognate tongue.
Or if that language yet with us abode.
Which Adam in the garden talked with God!
But our untempered speech descends—poor heirs!
Grimy and rough-cast still from Babel's bricklayers:
Curse on the brutish jargon we inherit,
Strong but to damn, not memorise, a spirit!
A cheek, a lip, a limb, a bosom, they
Move with light ease in speech of working-day;
And women we do use to praise even so.
But here the gates we burst, and to the temple go.
Their praise were her dispraise; who dare, who dare,
Adulate the seraphim for their burning hair?
How, if with them I dared, here should I dare it?
How praise the woman, who but know the spirit?
How praise the colour of her eyes, uncaught
While they were coloured with her varying thought
How her mouth's shape, who only use to know
What tender shape her speech will fit it to?
Or her lips' redness, when their joinèd veil
Song's fervid hand has parted till it wore them pale?

If I would praise her soul (temerarious if!),
All must be mystery and hieroglyph.
Heaven, which not oft is prodigal of its more
To singers, in their song too great before;

68

By which the hierarch of large poesy is
Restrained to his once sacred benefice;
Only for her the salutary awe
Relaxes and stern canon of its law;
To her alone concedes pluralities,
In her alone to reconcile agrees
The Muse, the Graces, and the Charities;
To her, who can the trust so well conduct
To her it gives the use, to us the usufruct.
What of the dear administress then may
I utter, though I spoke her own carved perfect way?
What of her daily gracious converse known,
Whose heavenly despotism must needs dethrone
And subjugate all sweetness but its own?
Deep in my heart subsides the infrequent word,
And there dies slowly throbbing like a wounded bird.
What of her silence, that outsweetens speech?
What of her thoughts, high marks for
mine own thoughts to reach?
Yet (Chaucer's antique sentence so to turn),
Most gladly will she teach, and gladly learn;
And teaching her, by her enchanting art,
The master threefold learns for all he can impart.
Now all is said, and all being said,—aye me!
There yet remains unsaid the very She.
Nay, to conclude (so to conclude I dare),
If of her virtues you evade the snare,
Then for her faults you'll fall in love with her.

Alas, and I have spoken of her Muse—
Her Muse, that died with her auroral dews!
Learn, the wise cherubim from harps of gold
Seduce a trepidating music manifold;
But the superior seraphim do know
None other music but to flame and glow.

So she first lighted on our frosty earth,
A sad musician, of cherubic birth,
Playing to alien ears—which did not prize
The uncomprehended music of the skies—
The exiled airs of her far Paradise.

But soon from her own harpings taking fire,
In love and light her melodies expire.
Now Heaven affords her, for her silenced hymn,
A double portion of the seraphim.

At the rich odours from her heart that rise,
My soul remembers its lost Paradise,
And antenatal gales blow from Heaven's shores of spice;
I grow essential all, uncloaking me
From this encumbering virility,
And feel the primal sex of heaven and poetry:
And parting from her, in me linger on
Vague snatches of Uranian antiphon.

How to the petty prison could she shrink
Of femineity?—Nay, but I think
In a dear courtesy her spirit would
Woman assume, for grace to womanhood.
Or, votaress to the virgin Sanctitude
Of reticent withdrawal's sweet, courted pale,
She took the cloistral flesh, the sexual veil,
Of her sad, aboriginal sisterhood;
The habit of cloistral flesh which founding Eve indued.

Thus do I know her: but for what men call
Beauty—the loveliness corporeal,
Its most just praise a thing unproper were
To singer or to listener, me or her.
She wears that body but as one indues

70

A robe, half careless, for it is the use;
Although her soul and it so fair agree,
We sure may, unattaint of heresy,
Conceit it might the soul's begetter be.
The immortal could we cease to contemplate,
The mortal part suggests its every trait.
God laid His fingers on the ivories
Of her pure members as on smoothèd keys,
And there out-breathed her spirit's harmonies
I'll speak a little proudly:—I disdain
To count the beauty worth my wish or gaze,
Which the dull daily fool can covet or obtain.
I do confess the fairness of the spoil,
But from such rivalry it takes a soil.
For her I'll proudlier speak:—how could it be
That I should praise the gilding on the psaltery?
'Tis not for her to hold that prize a prize,
Or praise much praise, though proudest in its wise,
To which even hopes of merely women rise.
Such strife would to the vanquished laurels yield,
Against *her* suffered to have lost a field.
Herself must with herself be sole compeer,
Unless the people of her distant sphere
Some gold migration send to melodise the year.

Yet I have felt what terrors may consort
In women's cheeks, the Graces' soft resort;
My hand hath shook at gentle hands' access,
And trembled at the waving of a tress;
My blood known panic fear, and fled dismayed,
Where ladies' eyes have set their ambuscade.
The rustle of a robe hath been to me
The very rattle of love's musketry;
Although my heart hath beat the loud advance,
I have recoiled before a challenging glance,

Proved gay alarms where warlike ribbons dance.
And from it all, this knowledge have I got,—
The whole that others have, is less than they have not;
All which makes other women noted fair,
Unnoted would remain and overshone in her.

How should I gauge what beauty is her dole,
Who cannot see her countenance for her soul;
As birds see not the casement for the sky?
And as 'tis check they prove its presence by,
I know not of her body till I find
My flight debarred the heaven of her mind.
Hers is the face whence all should copied be,
Did God make replicas of such as she;
Its presence felt by what it does abate,
Because the soul shines through tempered and mitigate:
Where—as a figure labouring at night
Beside the body of a splendid light—
Dark Time works hidden by its luminousness;
And every line he labours to impress
Turns added beauty, like the veins that run
Athwart a leaf which hangs against the sun.

There regent Melancholy wide controls;
There Earth- and Heaven-Love play for aureoles;
There Sweetness out of Sadness breaks at fits,
Like bubbles on dark water, or as flits
A sudden silver fin through its deep infinites;
There amorous Thought has sucked pale Fancy's breath,
And Tenderness sits looking toward the lands of death
There Feeling stills her breathing with her hand,
And Dream from Melancholy part wrests the wand
And on this lady's heart, looked you so deep,
Poor Poetry has rocked himself to sleep:
Upon the heavy blossom of her lips

Hangs the bee Musing; nigh her lids eclipse
Each half-occulted star beneath that lies;
And in the contemplation of those eyes,
Passionless passion, wild tranquillities.

EPILOGUE

TO THE POET'S SITTER

Wherein he excuseth himself for the manner of the Portrait.

Alas! now wilt thou chide, and say (I deem),
My figured descant hides the simple theme:
Or in another wise reproving, say
I ill observe thine own high reticent way.
Oh, pardon, that I testify of thee
What thou couldst never speak, nor others be!

Yet (for the book is not more innocent
Of what the gazer's eyes makes so intent),
She will but smile, perhaps, that I find my fair
Sufficing scope in such strait theme as her.
"Bird of the sun! the stars' wild honey-bee!
Is your gold browsing done so thoroughly?
Or sinks a singèd wing to narrow nest in me?"
(Thus she might say: for not this lowly vein
Out-deprecates her deprecating strain.)
Oh, you mistake, dear lady, quite; nor know
Ether was strict as you, its loftiness as low!

The heavens do not advance their majesty
Over their marge; beyond his empery
The ensigns of the wind are not unfurled,
His reign is hooped in by the pale o' the world.
'Tis not the continent, but the contained,
That pleasaunce makes or prison, loose or chained.

Too much alike or little captives me,
For all oppression is captivity.
What groweth to its height demands no higher;
The limit limits not, but the desire.

* * * * *

We, therefore, with a sure instinctive mind,
An equal spaciousness of bondage find
In confines far or near, of air or our own kind.
Our looks and longings, which affront the stars,
Most richly bruised against their golden bars,
Delighted captives of their flaming spears,
Find a restraint restrainless which appears
As that is, and so simply natural,
In you;—the fair detention freedom call,
And overscroll with fancies the loved prison-wall.

Such sweet captivity, and only such,
In you, as in those golden bars, we touch!
Our gazes for sufficing limits know
The firmament above, your face below;
Our longings are contented with the skies,
Contented with the heaven, and your eyes.
My restless wings, that beat the whole world through,
Flag on the confines of the sun and you;
And find the human pale remoter of the two.

AFTER HER GOING

The after-even! Ah, did I walk,
  Indeed, in her or even?
For nothing of me or around
  But absent She did leaven,
Felt in my body as its soul,
  And in my soul its heaven.

'Ah me! my very flesh turns soul,
  Essenced,' I sighed, 'with bliss!'
And the blackbird held his lutany,
  All fragrant-through with bliss;
And all things stilled were as a maid
  Sweet with a single kiss.

For grief of perfect fairness, eve
  Could nothing do but smile;
The time was far too perfect fair,
  Being but for a while;
And ah, in me, too happy grief
  Blinded herself with smile!

The sunset at its radiant heart
  Had somewhat unconfest:
The bird was loath of speech, its song
  Half-refluent on its breast,
And made melodious toyings with
  A note or two at best.

And she was gone, my sole, my Fair,

Ah, sole my Fair, was gone!
Methinks, throughout the world 'twere right
   I had been sad alone;
And yet, such sweet in all things' heart,
   And such sweet in my own!

MISCELLANEOUS POEMS

A FALLEN YEW

———————————

It seemed corrival of the world's great prime,
  Made to un-edge the scythe of Time,
    And last with stateliest rhyme.

No tender Dryad ever did indue
  That rigid chiton of rough yew,
    To fret her white flesh through:

But some god like to those grim Asgard lords,
  Who walk the fables of the hordes
    From Scandinavian fjords,

Upheaved its stubborn girth, and raised unriven,
  Against the whirl-blast and the levin,
    Defiant arms to Heaven.

When doom puffed out the stars, we might have said,
  It would decline its heavy head,
    And see the world to bed.

For this firm yew did from the vassal leas,
  And rain and air, its tributaries,
    Its revenues increase,

And levy impost on the golden sun,
   Take the blind years as they might run,
      And no fate seek or shun.

But now our yew is strook, is fallen—yea
   Hacked like dull wood of every day
      To this and that, men say.

Never!—To Hades' shadowy shipyards gone,
   Dim barge of Dis, down Acheron
      It drops, or Lethe wan.

Stirred by its fall—poor destined bark of Dis!—
   Along my soul a bruit there is
      Of echoing images,

Reverberations of mortality:
   Spelt backward from its death, to me
      Its life reads saddenedly.

Its breast was hollowed as the tooth of eld;
   And boys, their creeping unbeheld,
      A laughing moment dwelled.

Yet they, within its very heart so crept,
   Reached not the heart that courage kept
      With winds and years beswept.

And in its boughs did close and kindly nest
   The birds, as they within its breast,
      By all its leaves caressed.

But bird nor child might touch by any art
   Each other's or the tree's hid heart,

A whole God's breadth apart;

The breadth of God, he breadth of death and life!
  Even so, even so, in undreamed strife
    With pulseless Law, the wife,—

The sweetest wife on sweetest marriage-day,—
  Their souls at grapple in mid-way,
    Sweet to her sweet may say:

"I take you to my inmost heart, my true!"
  Ah, fool! but there is one heart you
    Shall never take him to!

The hold that falls not when the town is got,
  The heart's heart, whose immurèd plot
    Hath keys yourself keep not!

Its ports you cannot burst—you are withstood—
  For him that to your listening blood
    Sends precepts as he would.

Its gates are deaf to Love, high summoner;
  Yea, Love's great warrant runs not there:
    You are your prisoner.

Yourself are with yourself the sole consortress
  In that unleaguerable fortress;
    It knows you not for portress

Its keys are at the cincture hung of God;
  Its gates are trepidant to His nod;
    By Him its floors are trod.

And if His feet shall rock those floors in wrath,

Or blest aspersion sleek His path,
   Is only choice it hath.

Yea, in that ultimate heart's occult abode
   To lie as in an oubliette of God,
     Or as a bower untrod,
Built by a secret Lover for His Spouse;—
   Sole choice is this your life allows,
     Sad tree, whose perishing boughs
      So few birds house!

THE HOUND OF HEAVEN

I fled Him, down the nights and down the days;
　I fled Him, down the arches of the years;
I fled Him, down the labyrinthine ways
　　Of my own mind; and in the mist of tears
I hid from Him, and under running laughter.
　　　　Up vistaed hopes, I sped;
　　　　And shot, precipitated
Adown Titanic glooms of chasmed fears,
　　From those strong Feet that followed, followed after.
　　　　But with unhurrying chase,
　　　　And unperturbéd pace,
　　Deliberate speed, majestic instancy,
　　　　They beat—and a Voice beat
　　　　More instant than the Feet—
　　"All things betray thee, who betrayest Me."

　　　　I pleaded, outlaw-wise,
By many a hearted casement, curtained red,
　　Trellised with intertwining charities;
(For, though I knew His love Who followéd,
　　　　Yet was I sore adread
Lest, having Him, I must have naught beside)
But, if one little casement parted wide,
　　The gust of His approach would clash it to
　　Fear wist not to evade, as Love wist to pursue.
Across the margent of the world I fled,
　　And troubled the gold gateways of the stars,
　　Smiting for shelter on their changèd bars;
　　　　Fretted to dulcet jars

And silvern chatter the pale ports o' the moon.
I said to dawn: Be sudden—to eve: Be soon;
   With thy young skiey blossoms heap me over
     From this tremendous Lover!
Float thy vague veil about me, lest He see!
   I tempted all His servitors, but to find
My own betrayal in their constancy,
In faith to Him their fickleness to me,
   Their traitorous trueness, and their loyal deceit.
To all swift things for swiftness did I sue;
   Clung to the whistling mane of every wind.
     But whether they swept, smoothly fleet,
     The long savannahs of the blue;
      Or whether, Thunder-driven,
     They clanged his chariot 'thwart a heaven,
Plashy with flying lightnings round
the spurn o' their feet:—
   Fear wist not to evade as Love wist to pursue.
      Still with unhurrying chase,
      And unperturbèd pace,
    Deliberate speed, majestic instancy,
      Came on the following Feet,
      And a Voice above their beat—
   "Naught shelters thee, who wilt not shelter Me."

I sought no more that, after which I strayed,
   In face of man or maid;
But still within the little children's eyes
   Seems something, something that replies,
They at least are for me, surely for me!
I turned me to them very wistfully;
But just as their young eyes grew sudden fair
   With dawning answers there,
Their angel plucked them from me by the hair.
"Come then, ye other children, Nature's—share

With me" (said I) "your delicate fellowship;
    Let me greet you lip to lip,
    Let me twine with you caresses,
      Wantoning
    With our Lady-Mother's vagrant tresses,
      Banqueting
    With her in her wind-walled palace,
    Underneath her azured daïs,
    Quaffing, as your taintless way is,
      From a chalice
Lucent-weeping out of the dayspring."
      So it was done:
I in their delicate fellowship was one—
Drew the bolt of Nature's secrecies.
  I knew all the swift importings
  On the wilful face of skies;

  I knew how the clouds arise
  Spumèd of the wild sea-snortings;
    All that's born or dies
  Rose and drooped with—made them shapers
Of mine own moods, or wailful or divine—
  With them joyed and was bereaven.
  I was heavy with the even,
  When she lit her glimmering tapers
  Round the day's dead sanctities.
  I laughed in the morning's eyes.
I triumphed and I saddened with all weather,
    Heaven and I wept together,
And its sweet tears were salt with mortal mine;
Against the red throb of its sunset-heart
    I laid my own to beat,
    And share commingling heat;
But not by that, by that, was eased my human smart.
In vain my tears were wet on Heaven's grey cheek.

For ah! we know not what each other says,
   These things and I; in sound *I* speak—
Their sound is but their stir, they speak by silences.
Nature, poor stepdame, cannot slake my drouth;
   Let her, if she would owe me,
Drop yon blue bosom-veil of sky, and show me
   The breasts o' her tenderness:
Never did any milk of hers once bless
     My thirsting mouth.
     Nigh and nigh draws the chase,
     With unperturbèd pace,
   Deliberate speed majestic instancy
     And past those noisèd Feet
     A voice comes yet more fleet—
   "Lo! naught contents thee, who content'st not Me."

Naked I wait Thy love's uplifted stroke!
My harness piece by piece Thou hast hewn from me,
     And smitten me to my knee;
   I am defenceless utterly,
   I slept, methinks, and woke,
And, slowly gazing, find me stripped in sleep.
In the rash lustihead of my young powers,
   I shook the pillaring hours
And pulled my life upon me; grimed with smears,
I stand amid the dust o' the mounded years—
My mangled youth lies dead beneath the heap.
My days have crackled and gone up in smoke,
Have puffed and burst as sun-starts on a stream.
     Yea, faileth now even dream
The dreamer, and the lute the lutanist;
Even the linked fantasies, in whose blossomy twist
I swung the earth a trinket at my wrist,
Are yielding; cords of all too weak account
For earth with heavy griefs so overplussed.

Ah! is Thy love indeed
A weed, albeit an amaranthine weed,
Suffering no flowers except its own to mount?
        Ah! must—
        Designer infinite!—
Ah! must Thou char the wood ere Thou canst limn with it?

My freshness spent its wavering shower i' the dust;
And now my heart is as a broken fount,
Wherein tear-drippings stagnate, spilt down ever
        From the dank thoughts that shiver
Upon the sighful branches of my mind.
        Such is; what is to be?
The pulp so bitter, how shall taste the rind?
I dimly guess what Time in mists confounds;
Yet ever and anon a trumpet sounds
From the hid battlements of Eternity,
Those shaken mists a space unsettle, then
Round the half-glimpsèd turrets slowly wash again;
        But not ere him who summoneth
        I first have seen, enwound
With grooming robes purpureal, cypress-crowned;
His name I know, and what his trumpet saith.
Whether man's heart or life it be which yields
        Thee harvest, must Thy harvest fields
        Be dunged with rotten death?
            Now of that long pursuit
            Comes on at hand the bruit;
    That Voice is round me like a bursting sea:
        "And is thy earth so marred,
        Shattered in shard on shard?
    Lo, all things fly thee, for thou fliest Me!

    "Strange, piteous, futile thing!
Wherefore should any set thee love apart?

Seeing none but I makes much of naught" (He said),
"And human love needs human meriting:
 How hast thou merited—
Of all man's clotted clay the dingiest clot?
 Alack, thou knowest not
How little worthy of any love thou art!
Whom wilt thou find to love ignoble thee,
 Save Me, save only Me?
All which I took from thee I did but take,
 Not for thy harms,
But just that thou might'st seek it in My arms.
 All which thy child's mistake
Fancies as lost, I have stored for thee at home:
 Rise, clasp My hand, and come."

   Halts by me that footfall:
   Is my gloom, after all,
Shade of His hand, outstretched caressingly?
   "Ah, fondest, blindest, weakest,
   I am He Whom thou seekest!
Thou dravest love from thee, who dravest Me."

TO THE DEAD
CARDINAL OF WESTMINSTER

I will not perturbate
Thy Paradisal state
 With praise
 Of thy dead days;

To the new-heavened say,—
"Spirit, thou wert fine clay:"
 This do,
 Thy praise who knew.

Therefore my spirit clings
Heaven's porter by the wings,
 And holds
 Its gated golds

Apart, with thee to press
A private business;—
 Whence,
 Deign me audience.

Anchorite, who didst dwell
With all the world for cell
 My soul
 Round me doth roll

A sequestration bare.
Too far alike we were,

Too far
Dissimilar.

For its burning fruitage I
Do climb the tree o' the sky;
    Do prize
  Some human eyes.

You smelt the Heaven-blossoms,
And all the sweet embosoms
    The dear
  Uranian year.

Those Eyes my weak gaze shuns,
Which to the suns are Suns.
    Did
  Not affray your lid.

The carpet was let down
(With golden mouldings strown)
    For you
  Of the angels' blue.

But I, ex-Paradised,
The shoulder of your Christ
    Find high
  To lean thereby.

So flaps my helpless sail,
Bellying with neither gale,
    Of Heaven
  Nor Orcus even.

Life is a coquetry
Of Death, which wearies me,

Too sure
Of the amour;

A tiring-room where I
Death's divers garments try,
  Till fit
 Some fashion sit.

It seemeth me too much
I do rehearse for such
  A mean
 And single scene.

The sandy glass hence bear—
Antique remembrancer;
  My veins
 Do spare its pains.

With secret sympathy
My thoughts repeat in me
  Infirm
 The turn o' the worm

Beneath my appointed sod:
The grave is in my blood;
  I shake
 To winds that take

Its grasses by the top;
The rains thereon that drop
  Perturb
 With drip acerb

My subtly answering soul;
The feet across its knoll

Do jar
Me from afar.

As sap foretastes the spring;
As Earth ere blossoming
    Thrills
With far daffodils,

And feels her breast turn sweet
With the unconceivèd wheat;
    So doth
My flesh foreloathe

The abhorrèd spring of Dis,
With seething presciences
    Affirm
The preparate worm.

I have no thought that I,
When at the last I die,
    Shall reach
To gain your speech.

But you, should that be so,
May very well, I know,
    May well
To me in hell

With recognising eyes
Look from your Paradise—
    "God bless
Thy hopelessness!"

Call, holy soul, O call
The hosts angelical,

And say,—
"See, far away

"Lies one I saw on earth;
One stricken from his birth
    With curse
  Of destinate verse.

"What place doth He ye serve
For such sad spirit reserve,—
    Given,
  In dark lieu of Heaven,

"The impitiable Dæmon,
Beauty, to adore and dream on,
    To be
  Perpetually

"Hers, but she never his?
He reapeth miseries,
    Foreknows
  His wages woes;

"He lives detachèd days;
He serveth not for praise;
    For gold
  He is not sold;

"Deaf is he to world's tongue;
He scorneth for his song
    The loud
  Shouts of the crowd;

"He asketh not world's eyes;
Not to world's ears he cries;

Saith,—'These
Shut, if ye please;'

"He measureth world's pleasure,
World's ease as Saints might measure;
    For hire
  Just love entire

"He asks, not grudging pain;
And knows his asking vain,
    And cries—
  'Love! Love!' and dies;

"In guerdon of long duty,
Unowned by Love or Beauty;
    And goes—
  Tell, tell, who knows!

"Aliens from Heaven's worth,
Fine beasts who nose i' the earth,
    Do there
  Reward prepare.

"But are *his* great desires
Food but for nether fires?
    Ah me,
  A mystery!

"Can it be his alone,
To find when all is known,
    That what
  He solely sought

"Is lost, and thereto lost
All that its seeking cost?

That he
Must finally,

"Through sacrificial tears,
And anchoretic years,
　　Tryst
　With the sensualist?"

So ask; and if they tell
The secret terrible,
　　Good friend,
　I pray thee send

Some high gold embassage
To teach my unripe age.
　　Tell!
　Lest my feet walk hell.

A DEAD ASTRONOMER

(FATHER PERRY, S.J.)

Starry amorist, starward gone,
Thou art—what thou didst gaze upon!
Passed through thy golden garden's bars,
Thou seest the Gardener of the Stars.

She, about whose moonèd brows
Seven stars make seven glows,
Seven lights for seven woes;
She, like thine own Galaxy,
All lustres in one purity:—
What said'st thou, Astronomer,
When thou did'st discover*her*?
When thy hand its tube let fall,
Thou found'st the fairest Star of all!

A CORYMBUS FOR AUTUMN

Hearken my chant, 'tis
As a Bacchante's,
A grape-spurt, a vine-splash, a tossed
tress, flown vaunt 'tis!
Suffer my singing,
Gipsy of Seasons, ere thou go winging;
Ere Winter throws
His slaking snows
In thy feasting-flagon's impurpurate glows!
The sopped sun—toper as ever drank hard—
Stares foolish, hazed,
Rubicund, dazed,
Totty with thine October tankard.
Tanned maiden! with cheeks like apples russet,
And breast a brown agaric faint-flushing at tip,
And a mouth too red for the moon to buss it,
But her cheek unvow its vestalship;
Thy mists enclip
Her steel-clear circuit illuminous,
Until it crust
Rubiginous
With the glorious gules of a glowing rust.
Far other saw we, other indeed,
The crescent moon, in the May-days dead,
Fly up with its slender white wings spread
Out of its nest in the sea's waved mead!
How are the veins of thee, Autumn, laden?
Umbered juices,
And pulpèd oozes

Pappy out of the cherry-bruises,
Froth the veins of thee, wild, wild maiden!
 With hair that musters
 In globèd clusters,
 In tumbling clusters, like swarthy grapes,
Round thy brow and thine ears o'ershaden;
With the burning darkness of eyes like pansies,
 Like velvet pansies
 Wherethrough escapes
The splendid might of thy conflagrate fancies;
 With robe gold-tawny not hiding the shapes
 Of the feet whereunto it falleth down,
 Thy naked feet unsandallèd;
With robe gold-tawny that does not veil
 Feet where the red
 Is meshed in the brown,
Like a rubied sun in a Venice-sail.

The wassailous heart of the Year is thine!
His Bacchic fingers disentwine
 His coronal
 At thy festival;
His revelling fingers disentwine
 Leaf, flower, and all,
 And let them fall
Blossom and all in thy wavering wine.
The Summer looks out from her brazen tower,
 Through the flashing bars of July,
Waiting thy ripened golden shower;
 Whereof there cometh, with sandals fleet,
 The North-west flying viewlessly,
With a sword to sheer, and untameable feet,
 And the gorgon-head of the Winter shown
 To stiffen the gazing earth as stone.

In crystal Heaven's magic sphere
    Poised in the palm of thy fervid hand,
Thou seest the enchanted shows appear
That stain Favonian firmament;
Richer than ever the Occident
    Gave up to bygone Summer's wand.
Day's dying dragon lies drooping his crest,
Panting red pants into the West.
Or the butterfly sunset claps its wings
    With flitter alit on the swinging blossom,
The gusty blossom, that tosses and swings,
    Of the sea with its blown and ruffled bosom;
Its ruffled bosom wherethrough the wind sings
Till the crispèd petals are loosened and strown
        Overblown, on the sand;
        Shed, curling as dead
Rose-leaves curl, on the fleckèd strand.

Or higher, holier, saintlier when, as now,
All nature sacerdotal seems, and thou.
    The calm hour strikes on yon golden gong,
        In tones of floating and mellow light
    A spreading summons to even-song:
        See how there
        The cowlèd night
    Kneels on the Eastern sanctuary-stair.
What is this feel of incense everywhere?
    Clings it round folds of the blanch-amiced clouds,
Upwafted by the solemn thurifer,
    The mighty spirit unknown,
That swingeth the slow earth before
the embannered Throne?
    Or is't the Season under all these shrouds
Of light, and sense, and silence, makes her known
        A presence everywhere,

An inarticulate prayer,
A hand on the soothed tresses of the air?
But there is one hour scant
Of this Titanian, primal liturgy;
As there is but one hour for me and thee,
Autumn, for thee and thine hierophant,
Of this grave ending chant.
Round the earth still and stark
Heaven's death-lights kindle, yellow spark by spark,
Beneath the dreadful catafalque of the dark.

And I had ended there:
But a great wind blew all the stars to flare,
And cried, "I sweep the path before the moon!
Tarry ye now the coming of the moon,
For she is coming soon;"
Then died before the coming of the moon.
And she came forth upon the trepidant air,
In vesture unimagined-fair,
Woven as woof of flag-lilies;
And curdled as of flag-lilies
The vapour at the feet of her,
And a haze about her tinged in fainter wise.
As if she had trodden the stars in press,
Till the gold wine spurted over her dress,
Till the gold wine gushed out round her feet;
Spouted over her stainèd wear,
And bubbled in golden froth at her feet,
And hung like a whirlpool's mist round her.
Still, mighty Season, do I see't,
Thy sway is still majestical!
Thou hold'st of God, by title sure,
Thine indefeasible investiture,
And that right round thy locks are native to;
The heavens upon thy brow imperial,

This huge terrene thy ball,
And o'er thy shoulders thrown wide air's depending pall.
What if thine earth be blear and bleak of hue?
Still, still the skies are sweet!
Still, Season, still thou hast thy triumphs there!
How have I, unaware,
Forgetful of my strain inaugural,
Cleft the great rondure of thy reign complete,

Yielding thee half, who hast indeed the all?
I will not think thy sovereignty begun
But with the shepherd sun
That washes in the sea the stars' gold fleeces
Or that with day it ceases,
Who sets his burning lips to the salt brine,
And purples it to wine;
While I behold how ermined Artemis
Ordainèd weed must wear,
And toil thy business;
Who witness am of her,
Her too in autumn turned a vintager;
And, laden with its lampèd clusters bright,
The fiery-fruited vineyard of this night.

FROM
"THE MISTRESS OF VISION"

On Ararat there grew a vine,
When Asia from her bathing rose;
Our first sailor made a twine
Thereof for his prefiguring brows.
Canst divine
Where, upon our dusty earth, of that vine a cluster grows?

On Golgotha there grew a thorn
Round the long-prefigured Brows.
Mourn, O mourn!
For the vine have we the spine?Is this
   all the Heaven allows?

On Calvary was shook a spear;
Press the point into thy heart—
Joy and fear!
All the spines upon the thorn into curling tendrils start.

O, dismay!
I, a wingless mortal, sporting
With the tresses of the sun?
I, that dare my hand to lay
On the thunder in its snorting?
Ere begun,
Falls my singed song down the sky,
   even the old Icarian way.

From the fall precipitant
These dim snatches of her chant[2]
Only have remainèd mine;—
That from spear and thorn alone
May be grown
For the front of saint or singer any divinizing twine.

Her song said that no springing
Paradise but evermore
Hangeth on a singing
That has chords of weeping,
And that sings the after-sleeping
To souls which wake too sore.
'But woe the singer, woe!' she said; 'beyond
the dead his singing-lore,
All its art of sweet and sore,
He learns, in Elenore!'

Where is the land of Luthany,
Where is the tract of Elenore?
I am bound therefor.

'Pierce thy heart to find the key;
With thee take
Only what none else would keep;
Learn to dream when thou dost wake,
Learn to wake when thou dost sleep.
Learn to water joy with tears,
Learn from fears to vanquish fears;
To hope, for thou dar'st not despair,
Exult, for that thou dar'st not grieve;
Plough thou the rock until it bear;
Know, for thou else couldst not believe;
Lose, that the lost thou may'st receive;

Die, for none other way canst live.
When earth and heaven lay down their veil,
And that apocalypse turns thee pale;
When thy seeing blindeth thee
To what thy fellow-mortals see;
When their sight to thee is sightless;
Their living, death; their light, most lightless;
Search no more—
Pass the gates of Luthany, tread the region Elenore.'

Where is the land of Luthany,
And where the region Elenore?
I do faint therefor.

'When to the new eyes of thee
All things by immortal power,
Near or far,
Hiddenly
To each other linkèd are,
That thou canst not stir a flower
Without troubling of a star;
When thy song is shield and mirror
To the fair snake-curlèd Pain,
Where thou dar'st affront her terror
That on her thou may'st attain
Persean conquest; seek no more,
O seek no more!
Pass the gates of Luthany, tread the region Elenore.'

So sang she, so wept she,
Through a dream-night's day;
And with her magic singing kept she—
Mystical in music—
That garden of enchanting
In visionary May;

Swayless for my spirit's haunting,
Thrice-threefold walled with emerald
from our mortal mornings grey.

THE AFTER WOMAN

Daughter of the ancient Eve,
We know the gifts ye gave—and give.
Who knows the gifts which*you*shall give,
Daughter of the newer Eve?
You, if my soul be augur, you
Shall—O what shall you not, Sweet, do?
The celestial traitress play,
And all mankind to bliss betray;
With sacrosanct cajoleries
And starry treachery of your eyes,
Tempt us back to Paradise!
Make heavenly trespass;—ay, press in
Where faint the fledge-foot seraphin,
Blest Fool!Be ensign of our wars,
And shame us all to warriors!
Unbanner your bright locks,—advance
Girl, their gilded puissance,
I' the mystic vaward, and draw on
After the lovely gonfalon
Us to out-folly the excess
Of your sweet foolhardiness;
To adventure like intense
Assault against Omnipotence!

Give me song, as She is, new,
Earth should turn in time thereto!
New, and new, and thrice so new,
All old sweets, New Sweet, meant you!
Fair, I had a dream of thee,

When my young heart beat prophecy,
And in apparition elate
Thy little breasts knew waxèd great,
Sister of the Canticle,
And thee for God grown marriageable.
How my desire desired your day,
 That, wheeled in rumour on its way,
Shook me thus with presentience! Then
Eden's lopped tree shall shoot again:
For who Christ's eyes shall miss, with those
Eyes for evident nuncios?
Or who be tardy to His call
In your accents augural?
Who shall not feel the Heavens hid
Impend, at tremble of your lid,
And divine advent shine avowed
Under that dim and lucid cloud;
Yea, 'fore the silver apocalypse
Fail, at the unsealing of your lips?
When to love *you* is (O Christ's Spouse!)
To love the beauty of His house;
Then come the Isaian days; the old
Shall dream; and our young men behold
Vision—yea, the vision of Thabor mount,
Which none to other shall recount,
Because in all men's hearts shall be
The seeing and the prophecy.
For ended is the Mystery Play,
When Christ is life, and you the way;
When Egypt's spoils are Israel's right,
And Day fulfils the married arms of Night.
But here my lips are still.
Until
You and the hour shall be revealed,
This song is sung and sung not, and its words are sealed.

LINES

_____

TO W.M.

O tree of many branches! One thou hast
Thou barest not, but grafted'st on thee. Now,
Should all men's thunders break on thee, and leave
Thee reft of bough and blossom, that one branch
Shall cling to thee, my Father, Brother, Friend,
Shall cling to thee, until the end of end!

THE WAY OF A MAID

The lover, whose soul shaken is
In some decuman billow of bliss,
Who feels his gradual-wading feet
Sink in some sudden hollow of sweet,
And 'mid love's usèd converse comes
Sharp on a mood which all joy sums—
An instant fine compendium of
The liberal-leavèd writ of love—
His abashed pulses beating thick
At the exigent joy and quick,
Is dumbed, by aiming utterance great
Up to the miracle of his fate.
The wise girl, such Icarian fall
Saved by her confidence that she's small,—
As what no kindred word will fit
Is uttered best by opposite,
Love in the tongue of hate exprest,
And deepest anguish in a jest,—
Feeling the infinite must be
Best said by triviality,
Speaks, where expression bates its wings,
Just happy, alien, little things;
What of all words is in excess
Implies in a sweet nothingness,
With dailiest babble shows her sense
That full speech were full impotence;
And, while she feels the heavens lie bare,—
She only talks about her hair.

ODE TO
THE SETTING SUN

PRELUDE

The wailful sweetness of the violin
    Floats down the hushèd waters of the wind,
The heart-strings of the throbbing harp begin
    To long in aching music.Spirit-pined,

In wafts that poignant sweetness drifts, until
    The wounded soul ooze sadness.The red sun,
A bubble of fire, drops slowly toward the hill,
    While one bird prattles that the day is done.

O setting Sun, that as in reverent days
    Sinkest in music to thy smoothèd sleep,
Discrowned of homage, though yet crowned with rays,
    Hymned not at harvest more, though reapers reap:

For thee this music wakes not.O deceived,
    If thou hear in these thoughtless harmonies
A pious phantom of adorings reaved,
    And echo of fair ancient flatteries!

Yet, in this field where the Cross planted reigns,
    I know not what strange passion bows my head
To thee, whose great command upon my veins
    Proves thee a god for me not dead, not dead!

For worship it is too incredulous,
　For doubt—oh, too believing-passionate!
What wild divinity makes my heart thus
　A fount of most baptismal tears?—Thy straight

Long beam lies steady on the Cross.Ah me!
　What secret would thy radiant finger show?
Of thy bright mastership is this the key?
　Is*this*thy secret, then?And is it woe?

Fling from thine ear the burning curls, and hark
　A song thou hast not heard in Northern day;
For Rome too daring, and for Greece too dark,
　Sweet with wild wings that pass, that pass away!

ODE

Alpha and Omega, sadness and mirth,
　The springing music, and its wasting breath—
The fairest things in life are Death and Birth,
　And of these two the fairer thing is Death.
Mystical twins of Time inseparable,
　The younger hath the holier array,
　　And hath the awfuller sway:
　It is the falling star that trails the light,
　It is the breaking wave that hath the might,
The passing shower that rainbows maniple.
　Is it not so, O thou down-stricken Day,
That draw'st thy splendours round thee in thy fall?
High was thine Eastern pomp inaugural;
But thou dost set in statelier pageantry,
　Lauded with tumults of a firmament:
Thy visible music-blasts make deaf the sky,
　Thy cymbals clang to fire the Occident,
Thou dost thy dying so triumphally:

I *see* the crimson blaring of thy shawms!
  Why do those lucent palms
Strew thy feet's failing thicklier than their might,
Who dost but hood thy glorious eyes with night,
And vex the heels of all the yesterdays?
  Lo! this loud, lackeying praise
Will stay behind to greet the usurping moon,
 When they have cloud-barred over thee the West.
Oh, shake the bright dust from thy parting shoon!
 The earth not pæans thee, nor serves thy hest,
Be godded not by Heaven! avert thy face,
  And leave to blank disgrace
The oblivious world! unsceptre thee of state and place!

Ha! but bethink thee what thou gazedst on,
 Ere yet the snake Decay had venomed tooth;
The name thou bar'st in those vast seasons gone—
  Candid Hyperion,
 Clad in the light of thine immortal youth!
  Ere Dionysus bled thy vines,
 Or Artemis drave her clamours through the wood,
 Thou saw'st how once against Olympus' height
  The brawny Titans stood,
And shook the gods' world 'bout their ears, and how
Enceladus (whom Etna cumbers now)
 Shouldered me Pelion with its swinging pines,
The river unrecked, that did its broken flood
Spurt on his back: before the mountainous shock
 The rankèd gods dislock,
Scared to their skies; wide o'er rout-trampled night
Flew spurned the pebbled stars: those splendours then
 Had tempested on earth, star upon star
 Mounded in ruin, if a longer war
Had quaked Olympus and cold-fearing men.
  Then did the ample marge

And circuit of thy targe
Sullenly redden all the vaward fight,
Above the blusterous clash
Wheeled thy swung falchion's flash
And hewed their forces into splintered flight.

Yet ere Olympus thou wast, and a god!
Though we deny thy nod,
We cannot spoil thee of thy divinity.
What know we elder than thee?
When thou didst, bursting from the great void's husk,
Leap like a lion on the throat o' the dusk;
When the angels rose-chapleted
Sang each to other,
The vaulted blaze overhead
Of their vast pinions spread,
Hailing thee brother;
How chaos rolled back from the wonder,
And the First Morn knelt down to thy visage of thunder!
Thou didst draw to thy side
Thy young Auroral bride,
And lift her veil of night and mystery;
Tellus with baby hands
Shook off her swaddling-bands,
And from the unswathèd vapours laughed to thee.

Thou twi-form deity, nurse at once and sire!
Thou genitor that all things nourishest!
The earth was suckled at thy shining breast,
And in her veins is quick thy milky fire.
Who scarfed her with the morning? and who set
Upon her brow the day-fall's carcanet?
Who queened her front with the enrondured moon?
Who dug night's jewels from their vaulty mine
To dower her, past an eastern wizard's dreams,

When hovering on him through his haschish-swoon,
   All the rained gems of the old Tartarian line
Shiver in lustrous throbbings of tinged flame?
   Whereof a moiety in the Paolis' seams
   Statelily builded their Venetian name.
      Thou hast enwoofèd her
      An empress of the air,
And all her births are propertied by thee:
      Her teeming centuries
      Drew being from thine eyes:
Thou fatt'st the marrow of all quality.

Who lit the furnace of the mammoth's heart?
   Who shagged him like Pilatus' ribbèd flanks?
     Who raised the columned ranks
Of that old pre-diluvian forestry,
   Which like a continent torn oppressed the sea,
      When the ancient heavens did in rains depart,
      While the high-dancèd whirls
Of the tossed scud made hiss thy drenchèd curls?
     Thou rear'dst the enormous brood;
     Who hast with life imbued
The lion maned in tawny majesty,
     The tiger velvet-barred,
     The stealthy-stepping pard,
And the lithe panther's flexuous symmetry.

How came the entombèd tree a light-bearer,
     Though sunk in lightless lair?
     Friend of the forgers of earth,
   Mate of the earthquake and thunders volcanic,
   Clasped in the arms of the forces Titanic
     Which rock like a cradle the girth
      Of the ether-hung world;
Swart son of the swarthy mine,

When flame on the breath of his nostrils feeds
   How is his countenance half-divine,
   Like thee in thy sanguine weeds?
  Thou gavest him his light,
  Though sepultured in night
Beneath the dead bones of a perished world;
   Over his prostrate form
   Though cold, and heat, and storm,
The mountainous wrack of a creation hurled.
   Who made the splendid rose
   Saturate with purple glows;
Cupped to the marge with beauty; a perfume-press
   Whence the wind vintages
Gushes of warmèd fragrance richer far
   Than all the flavorous ooze of Cyprus' vats?
Lo, in yon gale which waves her green cymar,
    With dusky cheeks burnt red
    She sways her heavy head,
Drunk with the must of her own odorousness;
   While in a moted trouble the vexed gnats
Maze, and vibrate, and tease the noontide hush.
   Who girt dissolvèd lightnings in the grape?
Summered the opal with an Irised flush?
  Is it not thou that dost the tulip drape,
    And huest the daffodilly,
    Yet who hast snowed the lily,
And her frail sister, whom the waters name,
   Dost vestal-vesture 'mid the blaze of June,
   Cold as the new-sprung girlhood of the moon
Ere Autumn's kiss sultry her cheek with flame?
    Thou sway'st thy sceptred beam
    O'er all delight and dream,
  Beauty is beautiful but in thy glance:
    And like a jocund maid
    In garland-flowers arrayed,

Before thy ark Earth keeps her sacred dance.

And now, O shaken from thine antique throne,
   And sunken from thy coerule empery,
Now that the red glare of thy fall is blown
   In smoke and flame about the windy sky,
Where are the wailing voices that should meet
   From hill, stream, grove, and all of mortal shape
Who tread thy gifts, in vineyards as stray feet
   Pulp the globed weight of juiced Iberia's grape?
     Where is the threne o' the sea?
   And why not dirges thee
The wind, that sings to himself as he makes stride
   Lonely and terrible on the Andean height?
     Where is the Naiad 'mid her sworded sedge?
    The Nymph wan-glimmering
   by her wan fount's verge?
The Dryad at timid gaze by the wood-side?
    The Oread jutting light
   On one up-strainèd sole from the rock-ledge?
    The Nereid tip-toe on the scud o' the surge,
With whistling tresses dank athwart her face,
And all her figure poised in lithe Circean grace?
    Why withers their lament?
    Their tresses tear-besprent,
   Have they sighed hence with trailing garment-gem?
    O sweet, O sad, O fair!
    I catch your flying hair,
   Draw your eyes down to me, and dream on them!

A space, and they fleet from me. Must ye fade—
O old, essential candours, ye who made
   The earth a living and a radiant thing—
    And leave her corpse in our strained, cheated arms?
    Lo ever thus, when Song with chorded charms

Draws from dull death his lost Eurydice,
    Lo ever thus, even at consummating,
    Even in the swooning minute that claims her his,
    Even as he trembles to the impassioned kiss
    Of reincarnate Beauty, his control
    Clasps the cold body, and foregoes the soul!
        Whatso looks lovelily
Is but the rainbow on life's weeping rain.
Why have we longings of immortal pain,
And all we long for mortal? Woe is me,
And all our chants but chaplet some decay,
As mine this vanishing—nay, vanished Day.
The low sky-line dusks to a leaden hue,
    No rift disturbs the heavy shade and chill,
Save one, where the charred firmament lets through
    The scorching dazzle of Heaven; 'gainst which the hill,
        Out-flattened sombrely,
Stands black as life against eternity.
        Against eternity?
        A rifting light in me
Burns through the leaden broodings of the mind:
        O blessèd Sun, thy state
        Uprisen or derogate
Dafts me no more with doubt; I seek and find.

    If with exultant tread
        Thou foot the Eastern sea,
        Or like a golden bee
    Sting the West to angry red,
    Thou dost image, thou dost follow
        That King-Maker of Creation,
    Who, ere Hellas hailed Apollo,
        Gave thee, angel-god, thy station;
Thou art of Him a type memorial.
    Like Him thou hang'st in dreadful pomp of blood

Upon thy Western rood;
And His stained brow did veil like thine to night,
Yet lift once more Its light,
And, risen, again departed from our ball,
But when It set on earth arose in Heaven.
Thus hath He unto death His beauty given:
And so of all which form inheriteth
The fall doth pass the rise in worth;
For birth hath in itself the germ of death,
But death hath in itself the germ of birth.
It is the falling acorn buds the tree,
The falling rain that bears the greenery,
The fern-plants moulder when the ferns arise.
For there is nothing lives but something dies,
And there is nothing dies but something lives.
Till skies be fugitives,
Till Time, the hidden root of change, updries,
Are Birth and Death inseparable on earth;
For they are twain yet one, and Death is Birth.

AFTER-STRAIN

Now with wan ray that other sun of Song
Sets in the bleakening waters of my soul:
One step, and lo! the Cross stands gaunt and long
'Twixt me and yet bright skies, a presaged dole.

Even so, O Cross! thine is the victory.
Thy roots are fast within our fairest fields;
Brightness may emanate in Heaven from thee,
Here thy dread symbol only shadow yields.

Of reapèd joys thou art the heavy sheaf
Which must be lifted, though the reaper groan;
Yea, we may cry till Heaven's great ear be deaf,

118

But we must bear thee, and must bear alone.

Vain were a Simon; of the Antipodes
 Our night not borrows the superfluous day.
Yet woe to him that from his burden flees!
 Crushed in the fall of what he cast away.

Therefore, O tender Lady, Queen Mary,
 Thou gentleness that dost enmoss and drape
The Cross's rigorous austerity,
 Wipe thou the blood from wounds that needs must gape.

'Lo, though suns rise and set, but crosses stay,
 I leave thee ever,' saith she, 'light of cheer.'
'Tis so: yon sky still thinks upon the Day,
 And showers aërial blossoms on his bier.

Yon cloud with wrinkled fire is edgèd sharp;
 And once more welling through the air, ah me!
How the sweet viol plains him to the harp,
 Whose pangèd sobbings throng tumultuously.

Oh, this Medusa-pleasure with her stings!
 This essence of all suffering, which is joy!
I am not thankless for the spell it brings,
 Though tears must be told down for the charmed toy.

No; while soul, sky, and music bleed together,
 Let me give thanks even for those griefs in me,
The restless windward stirrings of whose feather
 Prove them the brood of immortality.
My soul is quitted of death-neighbouring swoon,
 Who shall not slake her immitigable scars
Until she hear 'My sister!' from the moon,
 And take the kindred kisses of the stars.

EPILOGUE TO
"A JUDGEMENT IN HEAVEN"

―――――――――――

Virtue may unlock hell, or even
A sin turn in the wards of Heaven,
(As ethics of the text-book go),
So little men their own deeds know,
Or through the intricate *mêlée*
Guess whitherward draws the battle-sway;
So little, if they know the deed,
Discern what therefrom shall succeed.
To wisest moralists 'tis but given
To work rough border-law of Heaven,
Within this narrow life of ours,
These marches 'twixt delimitless Powers.
Is it, if Heaven the future showed,
Is it the all-severest mode
To see ourselves with the eyes of God?
God rather grant, at His assize,
He see us not with our own eyes!

Heaven, which man's generations draws
Nor deviates into replicas,
Must of as deep diversity
In judgment as creation be.
There is no expeditious road
To pack and label men for God,
And save them by the barrel-load.
Some may perchance, with strange surprise,
Have blundered into Paradise.

In vasty dusk of life abroad,
They fondly thought to err from God,
Nor knew the circle that they trod;
And wandering all the night about,
Found them at morn where they set out.
Death dawned; Heaven lay in prospect wide:—
Lo! they were standing by His side!

GRACE OF THE WAY

The windy trammel of her dress,
   Her blown locks, took my soul in mesh;
God's breath they spake, with visibleness
   That stirred the raiment of her flesh:

And sensible, as her blown were,
   Beyond the precincts of her form
I felt the woman flow from her—
   A calm of intempestuous storm.

I failed against the affluent tide;
   Out of this abject earth of me
I was translated and enskied
   Into the heavenly-regioned She.

Now of that vision I bereaven
   This knowledge keep, that may not dim:—
Short arm needs man to reach to Heaven,
   So ready is Heaven to stoop to him.

Which sets, to measure of man's feet,
   No alien Tree for trysting-place;
And who can read, may read the sweet
   Direction in his Lady's face.

TO A SNOW-FLAKE

What heart could have thought you?—
Past our devisal
(O filigree petal!)
Fashioned so purely,
Fragilely, surely,
From what Paradisal
Imagineless metal,
Too costly for cost?
Who hammered you, wrought you,
From argentine vapour?—
'God was my shaper.
Passing surmisal,
He hammered, He wrought me,
From curled silver vapour,
To lust of His mind:—
Thou could'st not have thought me!
So purely, so palely,
Tinily, surely,
Mightily, frailly,
Insculped and embossed,
With His hammer of wind,
And His graver of frost.'

ORIENT ODE

Lo, in the sanctuaried East,
Day, a dedicated priest
In all his robes pontifical exprest,
Lifteth slowly, lifteth sweetly,
From out its Orient tabernacle drawn,
Yon orbèd sacrament confest
Which sprinkles benediction through the dawn;
And when the grave procession's ceased,
The earth with due illustrious rite
Blessed,—ere the frail fingers featly
Of twilight, violet-cassocked acolyte,
His sacerdotal stoles unvest—
Sets, for high close of the mysterious feast,
The sun in august exposition meetly
Within the flaming monstrance of the West.

God whom none may live and mark!
Borne within thy radiant ark,
While the Earth, a joyous David,
Dances before thee from the dawn to dark.
The moon, O leave, pale ruined Eve;
Behold her fair and greater daughter[3]
Offers to thee her fruitful water,
Which at thy first white Ave shall conceive!
Thy gazes do on simple her
Desirable allures confer;
What happy comelinesses rise
Beneath thy beautifying eyes!
Who was, indeed, at first a maid

Such as, with sighs, misgives she is not fair,
And secret views herself afraid,
Till flatteries sweet provoke the charms they swear:
Yea, thy gazes, blissful lover,
Make the beauties they discover!
What dainty guiles and treacheries caught
From artful prompting of love's artless thought
Her lowly loveliness teach her to adorn,
  When thy plumes shiver against the
      conscious gates of morn!

And so the love which is thy dower,
Earth, though her first-frightened breast
Against the exigent boon protest,
(For she, poor maid, of her own power
Has nothing in herself, not even love,
But an unwitting void thereof),
Gives back to thee in sanctities of flower;
And holy odours do her bosom invest,
That sweeter grows for being prest:
Though dear recoil, the tremorous nurse of joy,
From thine embrace still startles coy,
Till Phosphor lead, at thy returning hour,
The laughing captive from the wishing West.

Nor the majestic heavens less
Thy formidable sweets approve,
Thy dreads and thy delights confess,
That do draw, and that remove.
Thou as a lion roar'st, O Sun,
Upon thy satellites' vexèd heels;
Before thy terrible hunt thy planets run;
Each in his frighted orbit wheels,
Each flies through inassuageable chase,
Since the hunt o' the world begun,

The puissant approaches of thy face,
And yet thy radiant leash he feels.
Since the hunt o' the world begun,
Lashed with terror, leashed with longing,
The mighty course is ever run;
Pricked with terror, leashed with longing,
Thy rein they love, and thy rebuke they shun.
Since the hunt o' the world began,
With love that trembleth, fear that loveth,
Thou join'st the woman to the man;
And Life with Death
In obscure nuptials moveth,
Commingling alien, yet affinèd breath.

Thou art the incarnated Light
Whose Sire is aboriginal, and beyond
Death and resurgence of our day and night;
From him is thy vicegerent wand
With double potence of the black and white.
Giver of Love, and Beauty, and Desire,
The terror, and the loveliness, and purging,
The deathfulness and lifelness of fire!
Samson's riddling meanings merging
In thy twofold sceptre meet:
Out of thy minatory might,
Burning Lion, burning Lion,
Comes the honey of all sweet,
And out of thee, the eater, comes forth meat.
And though, by thine alternate breath,
Every kiss thou dost inspire
Echoeth
Back from the windy vaultages of death;
Yet thy clear warranty above
Augurs the wings of death too must
Occult reverberations stir of love

Crescent and life incredible;
That even the kisses of the just
Go down not unresurgent to the dust.
Yea, not a kiss which I have given,
But shall triúmph upon my lips in heaven,
Or cling a shameful fungus there in hell.
Know'st thou me not, O Sun? Yea, well
Thou know'st the ancient miracle,
The children know'st of Zeus and May;
And still thou teachest them, O splendent Brother,
To incarnate, the antique way,
The truth which is their heritage from their Sire
In sweet disguise of flesh from their sweet Mother.
My fingers thou hast taught to con
Thy flame-chorded psalterion,
Till I can translate into mortal wire—
Till I can translate passing well—
The heavenly harping harmony,
Melodious, sealed, inaudible,
Which makes the dulcet psalter of the world's desire.
Thou whisperest in the Moon's white ear,
And she does whisper into mine,—
By night together, I and she—
With her virgin voice divine,
The things I cannot half so sweetly tell
As she can sweetly speak, I sweetly hear.

By her, the Woman, does Earth live, O Lord,
Yet she for Earth, and both in thee.
Light out of Light!
Resplendent and prevailing Word
Of the Unheard!
Not unto thee, great Image, not to thee
Did the wise heathen bend an idle knee;
And in an age of faith grown frore

If I too shall adore,
Be it accounted unto me
A bright sciential idolatry!
God has given thee visible thunders
To utter thine apocalypse of wonders;
And what want I of prophecy,
That at the sounding from thy station
Of thy flagrant trumpet, see
The seals that melt, the open revelation?
Or who a God-persuading angel needs,
That only heeds
The rhetoric of thy burning deeds?
Which but to sing, if it may be,
In worship-warranting moiety,
So I would win
In such a song as hath within
A smouldering core of mystery,
Brimmèd with nimbler meanings up
Than hasty Gideons in their hands may sup;—
Lo, my suit pleads
That thou, Isaian coal of fire,
Touch from yon altar my poor mouth's desire,
And the relucent song take for thy sacred meeds.

To thine own shape
Thou round'st the chrysolite of the grape,
Bind'st thy gold lightnings in his veins;
Thou storest the white garners of the rains.
Destroyer and preserver, thou
Who medicinest sickness, and to health
Art the unthankèd marrow of its wealth;
To those apparent sovereignties we bow
And bright appurtenances of thy brow!
Thy proper blood dost thou not give,
That Earth, the gusty Mænad, drink and dance?

Art thou not life of them that live?
Yea, in glad twinkling advent, thou dost dwell
Within our body as a tabernacle!
Thou bittest with thine ordinance
The jaws of Time, and thou dost mete
The unsustainable treading of his feet.
Thou to thy spousal universe
Art Husband, she thy Wife and Church;
Who in most dusk and vidual curch,
Her Lord being hence,
Keeps her cold sorrows by thy hearse.
The heavens renew their innocence
And morning state
But by thy sacrament communicate:
Their weeping night the symbol of our prayers,
Our darkened search,
And sinful vigil desolate.

Yea, biune in imploring dumb,
Essential Heavens and corporal Earth await,
The Spirit and the Bride say: Come!
Lo, of thy Magians I the least
Haste with my gold, my incenses and myrrhs,
To thy desired epiphany, from the spiced
Regions and odorous of Song's traded East.
Thou, for the life of all that live
The victim daily born and sacrificed;
To whom the pinion of this longing verse
Beats but with fire which first thyself did give,
To thee, O Sun—or is't perchance, to Christ?

Ay, if men say that on all high heaven's face
The saintly signs I trace
Which round my stolèd altars hold their solemn place,
Amen, amen!For oh, how could it be,—

When I with wingèd feet had run
Through all the windy earth about,
Quested its secret of the sun,
And heard what thing the stars together shout,—
I should not heed thereout
Consenting counsel won:—
'By this, O Singer, know we if thou see.
When men shall say to thee: Lo! Christ is here,
When men shall say to thee: Lo! Christ is there,
Believe them: yea, and this—then art thou seer,
When all thy crying clear
Is but: Lo here! lo there!—ah me, lo everywhere!'

FROM "FROM THE NIGHT OF FOREBEING"

AN ODE AFTER EASTER

Castwide the folding doorways of the East,
For now is light increased!
And the wind-besomed chambers of the air,
See they be garnished fair;
And look the ways exhale some precious odours,
And set ye all about wild-breathing spice,
Most fit for Paradise.
Now is no time for sober gravity,
Season enough has Nature to be wise;
But now discinct, with raiment glittering free,
Shake she the ringing rafters of the skies
With festal footing and bold joyance sweet,
And let the earth be drunken and carouse!
For lo, into her house
Spring is come home with her world-wandering feet,
And all things are made young with young desires;
And all for her is light increased
In yellow stars and yellow daffodils,
And East to West, and West to East,
Fling answering welcome-fires,
By dawn and day-fall, on the jocund hills.
And ye, winged minstrels of her fair meinie,
Being newly coated in glad livery,
Upon her steps attend,
And round her treading dance and without end

Reel your shrill lutany.

What popular breath her coming does out-tell
The garrulous leaves among!
What little noises stir and pass
From blade to blade along the voluble grass!
O Nature, never-done
Ungaped-at Pentecostal miracle,
We hear thee, each man in his proper tongue!
Break, elemental children, break ye loose
From the strict frosty rule
Of grey-beard Winter's school.
Vault, O young winds, vault in your tricksome courses
Upon the snowy steeds that reinless use
In coerule pampas of the heaven to run;
Foaled of the white sea-horses,
Washed in the lambent waters of the sun.
Let even the slug-abed snail upon the thorn
Put forth a conscious horn!
Mine elemental co-mates, joy each one;
And ah, my foster-brethren, seem not sad—
No, seem not sad,
That my strange heart and I should be so little glad.
Suffer me at your leafy feast
To sit apart, a somewhat alien guest,
And watch your mirth,
Unsharing in the liberal laugh of earth;
Yet with a sympathy,
Begot of wholly sad and half-sweet memory—
The little sweetness making grief complete;
Faint wind of wings from hours that distant beat,
When I, I too,
Was once, O wild companions, as are you,
Ran with such wilful feet.

* * * * *

Hark to the *Jubilate* of the bird
For them that found the dying way to life!
And they have heard,
And quicken to the great precursive word;
Green spray showers lightly down the cascade of the larch;
The graves are riven,
And the Sun comes with power amid the clouds of heaven!
Before his way
Went forth the trumpet of the March;
Before his way, before his way
Dances the pennon of the May!
O earth, unchilded, widowed Earth, so long
Lifting in patient pine and ivy-tree
Mournful belief and steadfast prophecy,
Behold how all things are made true!
Behold your bridegroom cometh in to you,
Exceeding glad and strong.
Raise up your eyes, O raise your eyes abroad!
No more shall you sit sole and vidual,
Searching, in servile pall,
Upon the hieratic night the star-sealed sense of all:
Rejoice, O barren, and look forth abroad!
Your children gathered back to your embrace
See with a mother's face.
Look up, O mortals, and the portent heed;
In very deed,
Washed with new fire to their irradiant birth,
Reintegrated are the heavens and earth!
From sky to sod,
The world's unfolded blossom smells of God.

My little-worlded self! the shadows pass
In this thy sister-world, as in a glass,

Of all processions that revolve in thee:
Not only of cyclic Man
Thou here discern'st the plan,
Not only of cyclic Man, but of the cyclic Me.
Not solely of Mortality's great years
The reflex just appears,
But thine own bosom's year, still circling round
In ample and in ampler gyre
Toward the far completion, wherewith crowned,
Love unconsumed shall chant in his own furnace-fire.
How many trampled and deciduous joys
Enrich thy soul for joys deciduous still,
Before the distance shall fulfil
Cyclic unrest with solemn equipoise!
Happiness is the shadow of things past,
Which fools still take for that which is to be!
And not all foolishly:
For all the past, read true, is prophecy,
And all the firsts are hauntings of some Last,
And all the springs are flash-lights of one Spring.
Then leaf, and flower, and falless fruit
Shall hang together on the unyellowing bough;
And silence shall be Music mute
For her surchargèd heart. Hush thou!
These things are far too sure that thou should'st dream
Thereof, lest they appear as things that seem.

Nature, enough! within thy glass
Too many and too stern the shadows pass.
In this delighted season, flaming
For thy resurrection-feast,
Ah, more I think the long ensepulture cold,
Than stony winter rolled
From the unsealed mouth of the holy East;
The snowdrop's saintly stoles less heed

134

Than the snow-cloistered penance of the seed.
'Tis the weak flesh reclaiming
Against the ordinance
Which yet for just the accepting spirit scans.
Earth waits, and patient heaven,
Self-bonded God doth wait
Thrice-promulgated bans
Of his fair nuptial-date.
And power is man's,
With that great word of 'wait,'
To still the sea of tears,
And shake the iron heart of Fate.
In that one word is strong
An else, alas, much-mortal song;
With sight to pass the frontier of all spheres,
And voice which does my sight such wrong.

Not without fortitude I wait
The dark majestical ensuit
Of destiny, nor peevish rate
Calm-knowledged Fate.

     I do hear
From the revolving year
A voice which cries:
'All dies;
Lo, how all dies!O seer,
And all things too arise:
All dies, and all is born;
But each resurgent morn, behold,
more near the Perfect Morn.'

Firm is the man, and set beyond the cast
Of Fortune's game, and the iniquitous hour,
Whose falcon soul sits fast,

And not intends her high sagacious tour
Or ere the quarry sighted; who looks past
To slow much sweet from little instant sour,
And in the first does always see the last.

A COUNSEL OF MODERATION

On him the unpetitioned heavens descend,
Who heaven on earth proposes not for end;
The perilous and celestial excess
Taking with peace, lacking with thankfulness.
Bliss in extreme befits thee not, until
Thou'rt not extreme in bliss; be equal still:
Sweets to be granted think thyself unmeet
Till thou have learned to hold sweet not too sweet.

This thing not far is he from wise in art
Who teacheth; nor who doth, from wise in heart.

FROM
"ASSUMPTA MARIA"

——————————

'Thou needst not sing new songs,but say the old.'
—COWLEY.

Mortals, that behold a Woman,
  Rising 'twixt the Moon and Sun;
Who am I the heavens assume?an
  All am I,and I am one.

Multitudinous ascend I,
  Dreadful as a battle arrayed,
For I bear you whither tend I;
  Ye are I: be undismayed!
I, the Ark that for the graven
  Tables of the Law was made;
Man's own heart was one, one Heaven,
  Both within my womb were laid.
      For there Anteros with Eros
        Heaven with man conjoinèd was,—
      Twin-stone of the Law, *Ischyros*,
        Agios Athanatos.

I, the flesh-girt Paradises
  Gardenered by the Adam new,
Daintied o'er with sweet devices
  Which He loveth, for He grew.
I, the boundless strict savannah
  Which God's leaping feet go through;

I, the heaven whence the Manna,
   Weary Israel, slid on you!
      He the Anteros and Eros,
         I the body, He the Cross;
      He upbeareth me, *Ischyros*,
         Agios Athanatos!

I am Daniel's mystic Mountain,
   Whence the mighty stone was rolled;
I am the four Rivers' fountain,
   Watering Paradise of old;
Cloud down-raining the Just One am,
   Danae of the Shower of Gold;
I the Hostel of the Sun am;
   He the Lamb, and I the Fold.
      He the Anteros and Eros,
         I the body, He the Cross;
      He is fast to me, *Ischyros*,
         Agios Athanatos!

I, the presence-hall where Angels
   Do enwheel their placèd King—
Even my thoughts which, without change else,
   Cyclic burn and cyclic sing.
To the hollow of Heaven transplanted,
   I a breathing Eden spring,
Where with venom all outpanted
   Lies the slimed Curse shrivelling.
      For the brazen Serpent clear on
         That old fangèd knowledge shone;
      I to Wisdom rise, *Ischyron*,
         Agion Athanaton!

* * * * *

Then commanded and spake to me
  He who framed all things that be;
And my Maker entered through me,
  In my tent His rest took He.
Lo! He standeth, Spouse and Brother;
  I to Him, and He to me,
Who upraised me where my mother
  Fell, beneath the apple-tree.
      Risen 'twixt Anteros and Eros,
        Blood and Water, Moon and Sun,
      He upbears me, He*Ischyros*,
        I bear Him, the *Athanaton*!

Where is laid the Lord arisen?
  In the light we walk in gloom;
Though the sun has burst his prison,
  We know not his biding-room.
Tell us where the Lord sojourneth,
  For we find an empty tomb.
'Whence He sprung, there He returneth,
  Mystic Sun,—the Virgin's Womb.'
      Hidden Sun, His beams so near us,
        Cloud enpillared as He was
      From of old, there He,*Ischyros*,
        Waits our search, *Athanatos*.

Camp of Angels! Well we even
  Of this thing may doubtful be,—
If thou art assumed to Heaven,
  Or is Heaven assumed to thee!
      *Consummatum.*Christ the promised,
        Thy maiden realm is won, O Strong!
      Since to such sweet Kingdom comest,
        Remember me, poor Thief of Song!

Cadent fails the stars along:—
Mortals,that behold a woman
Rising 'twixt the Moon and Sun;
Who am I the heavens assume?an
All am I,and I am one.

FROM
"AN ANTHEM OF EARTH"

In nescientness, in nescientness,
Mother, we put these fleshly lendings on
Thou yield'st to thy poor children; took thy gift
Of life, which must, in all the after-days,
Be craved again with tears,—
With fresh and still-petitionary tears.
Being once bound thine almsmen for that gift,
We are bound to beggary, nor our own can call
The journal dole of customary life,
But after suit obsequious for't to thee.
Indeed this flesh, O Mother,
A beggar's gown, a client's badging,
We find, which from thy hands we simply took,
Nought dreaming of the after penury,
In nescientness.

In a little thought, in a little thought,
We stand and eye thee in a grave dismay,
With sad and doubtful questioning, when first
Thou speak'st to us as men: like sons who hear
Newly their mother's history, unthought
Before, and say—'She is not as we dreamed:
Ah me! we are beguiled!' What art thou, then,
That art not our conceiving? Art thou not
Too old for thy young children? Or perchance,
Keep'st thou a youth perpetual-burnishable
Beyond thy sons decrepit? It is long
Since Time was first a fledgling;

Yet thou may'st be but as a pendant bulla
Against his stripling bosom swung. Alack!
For that we seem indeed
To have slipped the world's great leaping-time, and come
Upon thy pinched and dozing days: these weeds,
These corporal leavings, thou not cast'st us new,
Fresh from thy craftship, like the lilies' coats,
But foist'st us off
With hasty tarnished piecings negligent,
Snippets and waste
From old ancestral wearings,
That have seen sorrier usage; remainder-flesh
After our father's surfeits; nay with chinks,
Some of us, that if speech may have free leave
Our souls go out at elbows. We are sad
With more than our sires' heaviness, and with
More than their weakness weak; we shall not be
Mighty with all their mightiness, nor shall not
Rejoice with all their joy. Ay, Mother! Mother!

What is this Man, thy darling kissed and cuffed,
Thou lustingly engender'st,
To sweat, and make his brag, and rot,
Crowned with all honour and all shamefulness?
From nightly towers
He dogs the secret footsteps of the heavens,
Sifts in his hands the stars, weighs them as gold-dust,
And yet is he successive unto nothing
But patrimony of a little mould,
And entail of four planks. Thou hast made his mouth
Avid of all dominion and all mightiness,
All sorrow, all delight, all topless grandeurs,
All beauty, and all starry majesties,
And dim transtellar things;—even that it may,
Filled in the ending with a puff of dust,

143

Confess—'It is enough.'The world left empty
What that poor mouthful crams.His heart is builded
For pride, for potency, infinity,
All heights, all deeps, and all immensities,
Arrased with purple like the house of kings,—
To stall the grey-rat, and the carrion-worm
Statelily lodge.Mother of mysteries!
Sayer of dark sayings in a thousand tongues,
Who bringest forth no saying yet so dark
As we ourselves, thy darkest!We the young,
In a little thought, in a little thought,
At last confront thee, and ourselves in thee,
And wake disgarmented of glory: as one
On a mount standing, and against him stands,
On the mount adverse, crowned with westering rays,
The golden sun, and they two brotherly
Gaze each on each;
He faring down
To the dull vale, his Godhead peels from him
Till he can scarcely spurn the pebble—
For nothingness of new-found mortality—
That mutinies against his gallèd foot.
Littly he sets him to the daily way,
With all around the valleys growing grave,
And known things changed and strange; but he holds on,
Though all the land of light be widowèd,
In a little thought.

In a little dust, in a little dust,
Earth, thou reclaim'st us, who do all our lives
Find of thee but Egyptian villeinage.
Thou dost this body, this enhavocked realm,
Subject to ancient and ancestral shadows;
Descended passions sway it; it is distraught
With ghostly usurpation, dinned and fretted

With the still-tyrannous dead; a haunted tenement,
Peopled from barrows and outworn ossuaries.
Thou giv'st us life not half so willingly
As thou undost thy giving; thou that teem'st
The stealthy terror of the sinuous pard,
The lion maned with curlèd puissance,
The serpent, and all fair strong beasts of ravin,
Thyself most fair and potent beast of ravin;
And thy great eaters thou, the greatest, eat'st.
Thou hast devoured mammoth and mastodon,
And many a floating bank of fangs,
The scaly scourges of thy primal brine,
And the tower-crested plesiosaure.
Thou fill'st thy mouth with nations, gorgest slow
On purple æons of kings; man's hulking towers
Are carcase for thee, and to modern sun
Disglutt'st their splintered bones.
Rabble of Pharaohs and Arsacidæ
Keep their cold house within thee; thou hast sucked down
How many Ninevehs and Hecatompyloi,
And perished cities whose great phantasmata
O'erbrow the silent citizens of Dis:—
Hast not thy fill?
Tarry awhile, lean Earth, for thou shalt drink,
Even till thy dull throat sicken,
The draught thou grow'st most fat on; hear'st thou not
The world's knives bickering in their sheaths?O patience!
Much offal of a foul world comes thy way,
And man's superfluous cloud shall soon be laid
In a little blood.

In a little peace, in a little peace,
Thou dost rebate thy rigid purposes
Of imposed being, and relenting, mend'st
Too much, with nought.The westering Phoebus' horse

Paws i' the lucent dust as when he shocked
The East with rising; O how may I trace
In this decline that morning when we did
Sport 'twixt the claws of newly-whelped existence,
Which had not yet learned rending? we did then
Divinely stand, not knowing yet against us
Sentence had passed of life, nor commutation
Petitioning into death.What's he that of
The Free State argues?Tellus! bid him stoop,
Even where the low*hic jacet*answers him;

Thus low, O Man! there's freedom's seignory,
Tellus' most reverend sole free commonweal,
And model deeply-policied: there none
Stands on precedence, nor ambitiously
Woos the impartial worm, whose favours kiss
With liberal largesse all; there each is free
To be e'en what he must, which here did strive
So much to be he could not; there all do
Their uses just, with no flown questioning.
To be took by the hand of equal earth
They doff her livery, slip to the worm,
Which lacqueys them, their suits of maintenance,
And that soiled workaday apparel cast,
Put on condition: Death's ungentle buffet
Alone makes ceremonial manumission;
So are the heavenly statutes set, and those
Uranian tables of the primal Law.
In a little peace, in a little peace,
Like fierce beasts that a common thirst makes brothers,
We draw together to one hid dark lake;
In a little peace, in a little peace,
We drain with all our burthens of dishonour
Into the cleansing sands o' the thirsty grave.
The fiery pomps, brave exhalations,

And all the glistering shows o' the seeming world,
Which the sight aches at, we unwinking see
Through the smoked glass of Death;
Death, wherewith's fined
The muddy wine of life; that earth doth purge
Of her plethora of man; Death, that doth flush
The cumbered gutters of humanity;
Nothing, of nothing king, with front uncrowned,
Whose hand holds crownets; playmate swart o' the strong;
Tenebrous moon that flux and refluence draws
Of the high-tided man; skull-housèd asp
That stings the heel of kings; true Fount of Youth,
Where he that dips is deathless; being's drone-pipe;
Whose nostril turns to blight the shrivelled stars,
And thicks the lusty breathing of the sun;
Pontifical Death, that doth the crevasse bridge
To the steep and trifid God; one mortal birth
That broker is of immortality.
Under this dreadful brother uterine,
This kinsman feared, Tellus, behold me come,
Thy son stern-nursed; who mortal-motherlike,
To turn thy weanlings' mouth averse, embitter'st
Thine over-childed breast.Now, mortal-sonlike,
I thou hast suckled, Mother, I at last
Shall sustenant be to thee.Here I untrammel,
Here I pluck loose the body's cementing,
And break the tomb of life; here I shake off
The bur o' the world, man's congregation shun,
And to the antique order of the dead
I take the tongueless vows: my cell is set
Here in thy bosom; my little trouble is ended
In a little peace.

CONTEMPLATION

This morning saw I, fled the shower,
The earth reclining in a lull of power:
The heavens, pursuing not their path,
Lay stretched out naked after bath,
Or so it seemed; field, water, tree, were still,
Nor was there any purpose on the calm-browed hill.

The hill, which sometimes visibly is
Wrought with unresting energies,
Looked idly; from the musing wood,
And every rock, a life renewed
Exhaled like an unconscious thought
When poets, dreaming unperplexed,
Dream that they dream of nought.
Nature one hour appears a thing unsexed,
Or to such serene balance brought
That her twin natures cease their sweet alarms,
And sleep in one another's arms.
The sun with resting pulses seems to brood,
And slacken its command upon my unurged blood.

The river has not any care
Its passionless water to the sea to bear;
The leaves have brown content;
The wall to me has freshness like a scent,
And takes half animate the air,
Making one life with its green moss and stain;
And life with all things seems too perfect blent
For anything of life to be aware.

The very shades on hill, and tree, and plain,
Where they have fallen doze, and where they doze remain.

No hill can idler be than I;
No stone its inter-particled vibration
Investeth with a stiller lie;
No heaven with a more urgent rest betrays
The eyes that on it gaze.
We are too near akin that thou shouldst cheat
Me, Nature, with thy fair deceit.
In poets floating like a water-flower
Upon the bosom of the glassy hour,
In skies that no man sees to move,
Lurk untumultuous vortices of power,
For joy too native, and for agitation
Too instant, too entire for sense thereof,
Motion like gnats when autumn suns are low,
Perpetual as the prisoned feet of love
On the heart's floors with painèd pace that go.
From stones and poets you may know,
Nothing so active is, as that which least seems so.

For he, that conduit running wine of song,
Then to himself does most belong,
When he his mortal house unbars
To the importunate and thronging feet
That round our corporal walls unheeded beat;
Till, all containing, he exalt
His stature to the stars, or stars
Narrow their heaven to his fleshly vault:
When, like a city under ocean,
To human things he grows a desolation,
And is made a habitation
For the fluctuous universe
To lave with unimpeded motion.

He scarcely frets the atmosphere
With breathing, and his body shares
The immobility of rocks;
His heart's a drop-well of tranquillity;
His mind more still is than the limbs of fear,
And yet its unperturbed velocity
The spirit of the simoom mocks.
He round the solemn centre of his soul
Wheels like a dervish, while his being is
Streamed with the set of the world's harmonies,
In the long draft of whatsoever sphere
He lists the sweet and clear
Clangour of his high orbit on to roll,
So gracious is his heavenly grace;
And the bold stars does hear,
Every one in his airy soar,
For evermore
Shout to each other from the peaks of space,
As thwart ravines of azure shouts the mountaineer.

CORRELATED GREATNESS

O nothing, in this corporal earth of man,
That to the imminent heaven of his high soul
Responds with colour and with shadow, can
Lack correlated greatness. If the scroll
Where thoughts lie fast in spell of hieroglyph
Be mighty through its mighty habitants;
If God be in His Name; grave potence if
The sounds unbind of hieratic chants;
All's vast that vastness means. Nay, I affirm
Nature is whole in her least things exprest,
Nor know we with what scope God builds the worm.
Our towns are copied fragments from our breast;
   And all man's Babylons strive but to impart
   The grandeurs of his Babylonian heart.

JULY FUGITIVE

Can you tell me where has hid her
   Pretty Maid July?
I would swear one day ago
   She passed by,
I would swear that I do know
   The blue bliss of her eye:
'Tarry, maid, maid,' I bid her;
   But she hastened by.
Do you know where she has hid her,
   Maid July?

Yet in truth it needs must be
   The flight of her is old;
Yet in truth it needs must be,
   For her nest, the earth, is cold.
No more in the poolèd Even
   Wade her rosy feet,
Dawn-flakes no more plash from them
   To poppies 'mid the wheat.
She has muddied the day's oozes
   With her petulant feet;
Scared the clouds that floated,
   As sea-birds they were,
Slow on the coerule
   Lulls of the air,
Lulled on the luminous
   Levels of air:
She has chidden in a pet
   All her stars from her;

Now they wander loose and sigh
   Through the turbid blue,
Now they wander, weep, and cry—
   Yea, and I too—
'Where are you, sweet July,
   Where are you?'

Who hath beheld her footprints,
   Or the pathway she goes?
Tell me, wind, tell me, wheat,
   Which of you knows?
Sleeps she swathed in the flushed Arctic
   Night of the rose?
Or lie her limbs like Alp-glow
   On the lily's snows?
Gales, that are all-visitant,
   Find the runaway;
And for him who findeth her
   (I do charge you say)
I will throw largesse of broom
   Of this summer's mintage,
I will broach a honey-bag
   Of the bee's best vintage.
Breezes, wheat, flowers sweet,
   None of them knows!
How then shall we lure her back
   From the way she goes?
For it were a shameful thing,
   Saw we not this comer
Ere Autumn camp upon the fields
   Red with rout of Summer.

When the bird quits the cage,
   We set the cage outside,
With seed and with water,

And the door wide,
Haply we may win it so
   Back to abide.
Hang her cage of earth out
   O'er Heaven's sunward wall,
Its four gates open, winds in watch
   By reinèd cars at all;
Relume in hanging hedgerows
   The rain-quenched blossom,
And roses sob their tears out
   On the gale's warm heaving bosom;
Shake the lilies till their scent
   Over-drip their rims;
That our runaway may see
   We do know her whims:
Sleek the tumbled waters out
   For her travelled limbs;
Strew and smoothe blue night thereon,
   There will—O not doubt her!—
The lovely sleepy lady lie,
   With all her stars about her!

ANY SAINT

His shoulder did I hold
Too high that I, o'erbold
    Weak one,
  Should lean thereon.

But He a little hath
Declined His stately path
    And my
  Feet set more high;

That the slack arm may reach
His shoulder, and faint speech
    Stir
  His unwithering hair.

And bolder now and bolder
I lean upon that shoulder
    So dear
  He is and near:

And with His aureole
The tresses of my soul
    Are blent
  In wished content.

Yes, this too gentle Lover
Hath flattering words to move her
    To pride
  By His sweet side.

Ah, Love! somewhat let be!
Lest my humility
   Grow weak
  When thou dost speak!

Rebate thy tender suit,
Lest to herself impute
   Some worth
  Thy bride of earth!

A maid too easily
Conceits herself to be
   Those things
  Her lover sings;

And being straitly wooed,
Believes herself the Good
   And Fair
  He seeks in her.

Turn something of Thy look,
And fear me with rebuke,
   That I
  May timorously

Take tremors in Thy arms,
And with contrivèd charms
   Allure
  A love unsure.

Not to me, not to me,
Builded so flawfully,
   O God,
  Thy humbling laud!

Not to this man, but Man,—
Universe in a span;
    Point
  Of the spheres conjoint;

In whom eternally
Thou, Light, dost focus Thee!—
    Didst pave
  The way o' the wave;

Rivet with stars the Heaven,
For causeways to Thy driven
    Car
  In its coming far

Unto him, only him;
In Thy deific whim
    Didst bound
  Thy works' great round

In this small ring of flesh;
The sky's gold-knotted mesh
    Thy wrist
  Did only twist

To take him in that net.—
Man! swinging-wicket set
    Between
  The Unseen and Seen;

Lo, God's two worlds immense,
Of spirit and of sense,
    Wed
  In this narrow bed;

Yea, and the midge's hymn
Answers the seraphim
    Athwart
  Thy body's court!

Great arm-fellow of God!
To the ancestral clod
    Kin,
  And to cherubin;

Bread predilectedly
O' the worm and Deity!
    Hark,
  O God's clay-sealed Ark,

To praise that fits thee, clear
To the ear within the ear,
    But dense
  To clay-sealed sense.

All the Omnific made
When in a word he said,
    (Mystery!)
  He uttered*thee*;

Thee His great utterance bore,
O secret metaphor
    Of what
  Thou dream'st no jot!

Cosmic metonymy!
Weak world-unshuttering key!
    One
  Seal of Solomon!

Trope that itself not scans
Its huge significance,
    Which tries
  Cherubic eyes.

Primer where the angels all
God's grammar spell in small,
    Nor spell
  The highest too well.

Point for the great descants
Of starry disputants;
    Equation
  Of creation.

Thou meaning, couldst thou see,
Of all which dafteth thee;
    So plain,
  It mocks thy pain;

Stone of the Law indeed,
Thine own self couldst thou read;
    Thy bliss
  Within thee is.

Compost of Heaven and mire,
Slow foot and swift desire!
    Lo,
  To have Yes, choose No;

Gird, and thou shalt unbind;
Seek not, and thou shalt find;
    To eat,
  Deny thy meat;

And thou shalt be fulfilled
With all sweet things unwilled:
     So best
   God loves to jest

With children small—a freak
Of heavenly hide-and-seek
     Fit
   For thy wayward wit,

Who art thyself a thing
Of whim and wavering;
     Free
   When His wings pen thee;

Sole fully blest, to feel
God whistle thee at heel;
     Drunk up
   As a dew-drop,

When He bends down, sun-wise,
Intemperable eyes;
     Most proud,
   When utterly bowed.

To feel thyself and be
His dear nonentity—
     Caught
   Beyond human thought

In the thunder-spout of Him,
Until thy being dim,
     And be
   Dead deathlessly.

Stoop, stoop; for thou dost fear
The nettle's wrathful spear,
    So slight
  Art thou of might!

Rise; for Heaven hath no frown
When thou to thee pluck'st down,
    Strong clod!
  The neck of God.

FROM
"THE VICTORIAN ODE"

_____

WRITTEN FOR THE QUEEN'S
GOLDEN JUBILEE DAY, 1897

Lo, in this day we keep the yesterdays,
And those great dead of the Victorian line.[4]
They passed, they passed, but cannot pass away,
For England feels them in her blood like wine.
She was their mother, and she is their daughter,
This Lady of the water,
And from their loins she draws the
    greatness which they were.
And still their wisdom sways,
Their power lives in her.
Their thews it is, England, that lift thy sword,
They are the splendour, England, in thy song,
They sit unbidden at thy council-board,
Their fame doth compass all thy coasts from wrong,
And in thy sinews they are strong.
Their absence is a presence and a guest
In this day's feast;
This living feast is also of the dead,
And this, O England, is thine All Souls' Day.
And when thy cities flake the night with flames,
Thy proudest torches yet shall be their names.

Come hither, proud and ancient East,
Gather ye to this Lady of the North,

And sit down with her at her solemn feast,
Upon this culminant day of all her days;
For ye have heard the thunder of her goings-forth,
And wonder of her large imperial ways.
Let India send her turbans, and Japan
Her pictured vests from that remotest isle
Seated in the antechambers of the Sun:
And let her Western sisters for a while
Remit long envy and disunion,
And take in peace
Her hand behind the buckler of her seas,
'Gainst which their wrath has splintered; come, for she
Her hand ungauntlets in mild amity.

Victoria! Queen, whose name is victory,
Whose woman's nature sorteth best with peace,
Bid thou the cloud of war to cease
Which ever round thy wide-girt empery
Fumes, like to smoke about a burning brand,
Telling the energies which keep within
The light unquenched, as England's light shall be;
And let this day hear only peaceful din.
For, queenly woman, thou art more than woman;
Thy name the often-struck barbarian shuns;
Thou art the fear of England to her foemen,
The love of England to her sons.
And this thy glorious day is England's; who
Can separate the two?
She joys thy joys and weeps thy tears,
And she is one with all thy moods;
Thy story is the tale of England's years,
And big with all her ills, and all her stately goods.
Now unto thee
The plenitude of the glories thou didst sow
Is garnered up in prosperous memory;

And, for the perfect evening of thy day,
An untumultuous bliss, serenely gay,
Sweetened with silence of the after-glow.

Nor does the joyous shout
Which all our lips give out
Jar on that quietude; more than may do
A radiant childish crew,
With well-accordant discord fretting the soft hour,
Whose hair is yellowed by the sinking blaze
Over a low-mouthed sea. Exult, yet be not twirled,
England, by gusts of mere
Blind and insensate lightness; neither fear
The vastness of thy shadow on the world.
If in the East
Still strains against its leash the unglutted beast
Of War; if yet the cannon's lip be warm;
Thou, whom these portents warn but not alarm,
Feastest, but with thy hand upon the sword,
As fits a warrior race.
Not like the Saxon fools of olden days,
With the mead dripping from the hairy mouth,
While all the South
Filled with the shaven faces of the Norman horde.

ST MONICA

At the Cross thy station keeping
With the mournful mother weeping,
Thou, unto the sinless Son,
Weepest for thy sinful one.
Blood and water from His side
Gush; in thee the streams divide:
From thine eyes the one doth start,
But the other from thy heart.

Mary, for thy sinner, see,
To her Sinless mourns with thee:
Could that Son the son not heed,
For whom two such mothers plead?
So thy child had baptism twice,
And the whitest from thine eyes.

The floods lift up, lift up their voice,
With a many-watered noise!
Down the centuries fall those sweet
Sobbing waters to our feet,
And our laden air still keeps
Murmur of a Saint that weeps.

Teach us but, to grace our prayers,
Such divinity of tears,—
Earth should be lustrate again
With contrition of that rain:
Till celestial floods o'er rise
The high tops of Paradise.

TO THE
SINKING SUN

How graciously thou wear'st the yoke
   Of use that does not fail!
The grasses, like an anchored smoke,
   Ride in the bending gale;
This knoll is snowed with blosmy manna,
   And fire-dropt as a seraph's mail.

Here every eve thou stretchest out
   Untarnishable wing,
And marvellously bring'st about
   Newly an olden thing;
Nor ever through like-ordered heaven
   Moves largely thy grave progressing.

Here every eve thou goest down
   Behind the self-same hill,
Nor ever twice alike go'st down
   Behind the self-same hill;
Nor like-ways is one flame-sopped flower
   Possessed with glory past its will.

Not twice alike! I am not blind,
   My sight is live to see;
And yet I do complain of thy
   Weary variety.
O Sun! I ask thee less or more,
   Change not at all, or utterly!

O give me unprevisioned new,
    Or give to change reprieve!
For new in me is olden too,
    That I for sameness grieve.
O flowers! O grasses! be but once
    The grass and flower of yester-eve!

Wonder and sadness are the lot
    Of change: thou yield'st mine eyes
Grief of vicissitude, but not
    Its penetrant surprise.
Immutability mutable
    Burthens my spirit and the skies.

O altered joy, all joyed of yore,
    Plodding in unconned ways!
O grief grieved out, and yet once more
    A dull, new, staled amaze!
I dream, and all was dreamed before,
    Or dream I so? the dreamer says.

DREAM-TRYST

The breaths of kissing night and day
  Were mingled in the eastern Heaven:
Throbbing with unheard melody
  Shook Lyra all its star-chord seven:
    When dusk shrunk cold, and light trod shy,
      And dawn's grey eyes were troubled grey;
    And souls went palely up the sky,
      And mine to Lucidé.

There was no change in her sweet eyes
  Since last I saw those sweet eyes shine;
There was no change in her deep heart
  Since last that deep heart knocked at mine.
    Her eyes were clear, her eyes were Hope's,
      Wherein did ever come and go
    The sparkle of the fountain-drops
      From her sweet soul below.

The chambers in the house of dreams
  Are fed with so divine an air,
That Time's hoar wings grow young therein,
  And they who walk there are most fair.
    I joyed for me, I joyed for her,
      Who with the Past meet girt about:
    Where our last kiss still warms the air,
      Nor can her eyes go out.

BUONA NOTTE

Jane Williams, in her last letter to Shelley, wrote: "Why do you talk of never enjoying moments like the past? Are you going to join your friend Plato, or do you expect I shall do so soon? Buona Notte." That letter was dated July 6th; Shelley was drowned on the 8th; and this is his imagined reply to it from another world:—

Ariel to Miranda:—hear
This good-night the sea-winds bear;
And let thine unacquainted ear
Take grief for their interpreter.
Good-night; I have risen so high
Into slumber's rarity,
Not a dream can beat its feather
Through the unsustaining ether.
Let the sea-winds make avouch
How thunder summoned me to couch,
Tempest curtained me about
And turned the sun with his own hand out:
And though I toss upon my bed
My dream is not disquieted;
Nay, deep I sleep upon the deep,
And my eyes are wet, but I do not weep;
And I fell to sleep so suddenly
That my lips are moist yet—could'st thou see—
With the good-night draught I have drunk to thee.
Thou can'st not wipe them; for it was Death
Damped my lips that has dried my breath.
A little while—it is not long—
The salt shall dry on them like the song.

Now know'st thou, that voice desolate,
Mourning ruined joy's estate,
Reached thee through a closing gate.
"Go'st thou to Plato?" Ah, girl, no!
It is to Pluto that I go.

ARAB LOVE SONG

The hunchèd camels of the night [5]
Trouble the bright
And silver waters of the moon.
The Maiden of the Morn will soon
Through Heaven stray and sing,
Star gathering.
Now while the dark about our loves is strewn,
Light of my dark, blood of my heart, O come!
And night will catch her breath up, and be dumb.

Leave thy father, leave thy mother
And thy brother;
Leave the black tents of thy tribe apart!
Am I not thy father and thy brother,
And thy mother?
And thou—what needest with thy tribe's black tents
Who hast the red pavilion of my heart?

THE KINGDOM OF GOD

"IN NO STRANGE LAND"

O World Invisible, we view thee,
O World intangible, we touch thee,
O World unknowable, we know thee,
Inapprehensible, we clutch thee!

Does the fish soar to find the ocean,
The eagle plunge to find the air—
That we ask of the stars in motion
If they have rumour of thee there?

Not where the wheeling systems darken,
And our benumbed conceiving soars!—
The drift of pinions, would we hearken,
Beats at our own clay-shuttered doors.

The angels keep their ancient places;—
Turn but a stone, and start a wing!
'Tis ye, 'tis your estrangèd faces,
That miss the many-splendoured thing.

But (when so sad thou canst not sadder)
Cry;—and upon thy so sore loss
Shall shine the traffic of Jacob's ladder
Pitched betwixt Heaven and Charing Cross.

Yea, in the night, my Soul, my daughter,

Cry,—clinging Heaven by the hems;
And lo, Christ walking on the water,
Not of Genesareth, but Thames! [6]

ENVOY

Go, songs, for ended is our brief, sweet play;
Go, children of swift joy and tardy sorrow:
And some are sung, and that was yesterday,
And some unsung, and that may be to-morrow.
Go forth; and if it be o'er stony way,
Old joy can lend what newer grief must borrow:
And it was sweet, and that was yesterday,
And sweet is sweet, though purchasèd with sorrow.
Go, songs, and come not back from your far way;
And if men ask you why ye smile and sorrow,
Tell them ye grieve, for your hearts know To-day,
Tell them ye smile, for your eyes know To-morrow.

APPRECIATIONS

OF
FRANCIS THOMPSON

"Such pronouncements proved at least that a poet,
who had no friend save such as his published poems
gained for him, could count on an immediate
recognition for high merit. For these tributes, and
many more of like welcoming, placed him instantly
out of range of the common casualties of criticism."
— FROM *Note on Francis Thompson, p. xii.*

As the writer of the "Note" has not attempted a critical estimate
of the poetry, some of these Appreciations, forming a part of the
poet's life-history and even of the literary history of his time, are
here reproduced.

Mr Francis Thompson is a writer whom it is impossible that
any qualified judge should deny to be a "new poet." And while
most poets of his quality have usually to wait a quarter of a
century or more for adequate recognition, this poet is pretty
sure of a wide and immediate acknowledgement.... We find
that in these poems profound thought, far-fetched splendour
of imagery, and nimble-witted discernment of those analogies
which are the roots of the poet's language, abound ... qualities

which ought to place him in the permanent ranks of fame, with Cowley and with Crashaw.... *The Hound of Heaven* has so great and passionate and such a metre-creating motive, that we are carried over all obstructions of the rhythmical current, and are compelled to pronounce it, at the end, one of the very few "great" odes of which the language can boast. In a lesser degree this metre-making passion prevails in the seven remarkable pieces called *Love in Dian's Lap*, poems of which Laura might have been proud, and Lucretia not ashamed, to have had addressed to her. The main region of Mr Thompson's poetry is the inexhaustible and hitherto almost unworked mine of Catholic philosophy. Not but that he knows better than to make his religion the direct subject of any of his poems, unless it presents itself to him as a human passion, and the most human of passions, as it does in the splendid ode just noticed, in which God's long pursuit and final conquest of the resisting soul is described in a torrent of as humanly impressive verse as was ever inspired by a natural affection. Mr Thompson places himself, by these poems, in the front rank of the pioneers of the movement which, if it be not checked, as in the history of the world it has once or twice been checked before, by premature formulation and by popular and profane perversion, must end in creating a "new heaven and a new earth."

—COVENTRY PATMORE,
The Fortnightly Review.

It is not only the religious ecstasy of Crashaw that they recall; for all the daringly fantastic imagery, all the love-lyrical hyperbole, all that strange mixture and artifice, of spontaneous passion and studied conceit, which were so characteristic of the age of Crashaw, are with the same astonishing fidelity reproduced. Where, unless, perhaps, in here and there a sonnet of Rossetti's, has this sort of sublimated enthusiasm for the bodily and spiritual beauty of womanhood found such expression as in *Love in Dian's Lap* between the age of the Stuarts and our own? To realize the full extent to which the religious, or semi-religious, emotions—now ecstatic, now awe-stricken—dominate and colour the entire fabric of these strange poems, they must be read throughout. In the lines *To the Dead Cardinal of Westminster* we see them at their subtlest; and in the very powerful piece, *The Hound of Heaven*—a poem setting forth the pursuit of the human soul by divine grace—they are at their most intense.... That minority who can recognize the essentials under the accidents of poetry, and who feel that it is to poetic Form alone, and not to forms, that eternity belongs, will agree that, alike in wealth and dignity of imagination, in depth and subtlety of thought, and in magic and mastery of language, a new poet of the first rank is to be welcomed in the author of this volume.

—H. D. TRAILL,
The Nineteenth Century.

The first thing to be done, and by far the most important, is to recognize that we are here face to face with a poet of the first order, a man of imagination all compact, a seer and singer of rare genius. He revels indeed in "orgiac imageries," and revelry implies excess. But when excess is an excess of strength, the debauch a debauch of beauty, who can condemn or even regret it? Would we had a few more poets who could exceed in such imagery as this! It is no minor Caroline singer he recalls, but the Jacobean Shakespeare.

—THE DAILY CHRONICLE.

A volume of poetry has not appeared in Queen Victoria's reign more authentic in greatness of utterance than this. In the rich and virile harmonies of his line, in strange and lovely vision, in fundamental meaning, he is possibly the first of Victorian poets, and at least is he of none the inferior.... In all sobriety do we believe him of all poets to be the most celestial in vision, the most august in faculty.... In a word, a new planet has swum into the ken of the watchers of the poetic skies. These are big words; but we have weighed them. For there is that in Mr Francis Thompson's poetry which discourages the flamboyant appreciations of the more facile impressionist, and gives him pause in his ready-made enthusiasms. It is patent on the first page that there is genius in this inspiration, and the great note in this utterance; but page after page reveals the rich and the strange, and the richer and the stranger in so many original moods and noble measures, that the reviewer feels the necessity of caution.... In nothing does Thompson appear more authentically a poet than in the fact that his sense of beauty is part of his religion. In this he is like Shelley, except that Shelley's sense of beauty was his religion, and lived in an atmosphere of sensuousness, a sensuousness that has little of the grosser taints of earth about it indeed, but which is still sensuousness. Therefore, Shelley wrote the glorious *Epipsychidion*; therefore, Mr Thompson writes *Her Portrait*, the longest and greatest poem in his book; and, speaking for ourselves, we shall say at once that *Epipsychidion*, long unique in the language, has at last found its parallel, perhaps its peer, in *Her Portrait*. Of this "Her" of Mr Thompson's we must say that she is the significance of his book. If his sense of beauty is part of his religion, his religion is that of a rapt Catholic, to whom the very heaven, with all that therein be, is open and palpable; his is the Catholicism of profound mysticism, and of the most universal temper.... It is perfectly safe to affirm that if Mr Thompson write no other line, by this volume alone he is as secure of remembrance as any poet of the century. His vocabulary is very great.... Mr Thompson's first volume is no mere promise—it is itself among the great achievements of English poetry; it has reached the peak of Parnassus at a bound.

He has actually accomplished the high thing in metaphysical poetry that Donne and Crashaw only dreamed of. His mysticism is infinitely more profound and significant than theirs, as his imagination is more impulsive, ardent, and beautiful. He is the great Platonist of English poetry. If Mr Thompson had never written anything after his first volume, there would be but one

Stuart poet with whom the author of *Her Portrait* could be compared for orchestral majesties of song, and that one Milton.... He is an argonaut of literature, far travelled in the realms of gold, and he has in a strange degree the assimilative mind.... We do not think we forget any of the splendid things of an English anthology when we say that *The Hound of Heaven* seems to us, on the whole, the most wonderful lyric in the language. It fingers all the stops of the spirit, and we hear now a thrilling and dolorous note of doom, and now the quiring of the spheres, and now the very pipes of Pan, but under all the still, sad music of humanity. It is the return of the nineteenth century to Thomas a Kempis.

—J. L. GARVIN,
The Newcastle Chronicle and The Bookman.

The fine frenzy, and the fine line: these are two root characteristics of Mr Thompson's really remarkable poem. One has seldom seen poet more wildly abandoned to his rapture, more absorbed in the trance of his ecstasy. When the irresistible moment comes, he throws himself upon his mood as a glad swimmer gives himself to the waves, careless whither the strong tide carries him, knowing only the wild joy of the laughing waters and the rainbow spray. He shouts, as it were, for mere gladness, in the welter of wonderful words, and he dives swift and fearless to fetch his deep-sea fancies. When weak men venture on these vagaries they drown; but Mr Thompson is a strong swimmer. Hyperboles, which in other hands had seemed merely absurd, in his delight us as examples of that "fine excess" which is one of the most enthralling of the many enchantments of poetry.... Indeed, Mr Thompson must simply be Crashaw born again, but born greater. Though the conception, for example, of *The Hound of Heaven*—the case of a sinner fleeing from the love of Christ— is exactly in Crashaw's vein, yet it was not in his power to have suggested such tremendous speed and terror of flight as whirls through every line of Mr Thompson's poem.

—R. LE GALLIENNE,
The Daily Chronicle.

A new poet—and this time a major and not a minor one. On the section called *Love in Dian's Lap*, much might be said of its extraordinary conception and workmanship. The section is one long, beautiful song of praise, and even worship, of one whom the poet calls his "dear administress." But surely never was woman worshipped with more utter chastity of passion. Whether *Before her Portrait in Youth*, or regarding her as *A poet breaking silence*, or only reflecting on her wearing of a new dress, the Poet is so full of fine matter and so adoring in his expression of it, as to bring Dante himself to mind.

—*St. James's Gazette.*

Here are dominion—domination over language, and a sincerity as of Robert Burns.... The epithet sublime has been sadly stained and distorted by comic writers, and there is a danger in applying it in its honest light without warning. This safeguard established, we have to say that in our opinion Mr Thompson's poetry at its highest attains a sublimity unsurpassed by any Victorian poet—a sublimity which will stand the hideous test of extracts. In *Her Portrait* a constant interchange of symbol between earthly and heavenly beauty pulses like day and night.

—JOHN DAVIDSON,
The Speaker.

When at the end of 1893 there appeared a little quarto volume of poems by Francis Thompson, the English world of letters experienced an agreeable shock of surprise. It was as if a rocket had been sent up into a dark night. His poems have all the "pomp and prodigality" of imagination for which Gray's frugal muse longed.

—*The Spectator.*

Words and cadences must have had an intoxication for him, the intoxication of the scholar; and "cloudy trophies" were continually falling into his hands, and half through them, in his hurry to seize and brandish them. He swung a rare incense in a censer of gold, under the vault of a chapel where he had hung votive offerings. When he chanted in his chapel of dreams, the airs were often airs which he had learnt from Crashaw and from Patmore. They came to life again when he used them, and he made for himself a music which was part strangely familiar and part his own, almost bewilderingly. Such reed-notes and such orchestration of sound were heard nowhere else; and people listened to the music, entranced as by a new magic. The genius of Francis Thompson was Oriental, exuberant in colour, woven into elaborate patterns, and went draped in old silk robes, that had survived many dynasties. The spectacle of him was an enchantment; he passed like a wild vagabond of the mind, dazzling our sight. He had no message, but he dropt sentences by the way, cries of joy or pity, love of children, worship of the Virgin and the Saints, and of those who were patron saints to him on earth; his voice was heard like a wandering music, which no one heeded for what it said, in a strange tongue, but which came troublingly into the mind, bringing it the solace of its old, recaptured melodies.

—ARTHUR SYMONS,
The Saturday Review.

To read Mr Francis Thompson's *Poems*, then, is like setting sail with Drake or Hawkins in search of new worlds and golden spoils. He has the magnificent Elizabethan manner, the splendour of conception, the largeness of imagery.

—KATHERINE TYNAN-HINKSON,
The Bookman.

As a matter of fact—such fact as one kisses the book to in a court of law—it was in a railway carriage on my way back to London that I first read Mr Thompson's poem, *The Mistress of Vision*; but, in such truth as would pass anywhere but in a court of law, it was at Cambridge, in the height of the summer term and in a Fellows' Garden that the revelation first came. I thought then in my enthusiasm that no such poem had been written or attempted since Coleridge attempted, and left off writing, *Kubla Khan*. In a cooler hour I think so yet; and, were my age twenty-five or so, it would delight me to swear to it, riding to any man's drawbridge who shuts his gates against it, and blowing the horn of challenge. It is verily a wonderful poem; hung, like a fairy tale, in middle air—a sleeping palace of beauty set in a glade in the heart of the woods of Westermain, surprised there and recognized with a gasp as satisfying, and summarizing a thousand youthful longings after beauty. To me also my admiration seemed too hot to last; but four or five years leave me unrepentant. It seemed to me to be more likely to be a perishable joy, because I had once clutched at, and seemed to grasp, similar beauties in Poe. Mr Thompson's thought, always strong, often runs into phrases of exquisite sweetness and exquisite clarity.... The lines beginning:

> "Firm is the man, and set beyond the cast
> Of fortune's game and the iniquitous hour,"

are worthy to be remembered beside Daniel's *Epistle to the Countess of Cumberland*.

> —Sir A. Quiller Couch ("Q"),
> *The Daily News.*

Thompson's poetry is a "wassail of orgiac imageries." He is a poet's poet, like Shelley and Blake. In order to follow him as he soars from image to image and symbol to symbol, you must have the rare wings of imagination.... Thompson mixes his metaphors so wisely that they illumine each other, strange light shooting out of their weltering chaos, like the radiance of phosphorescent waves. He troubles you with sudden pictures that flash out against the blackness. This gift of dreadful vision is not found in Crashaw or in Patmore, in Donne or in Herbert, and therefore it seems to me that Thompson is essentially more akin to Blake,

Coleridge and Rossetti than to the ecclesiastical mystics. He is a twentieth-century mystic with a seventeenth-century manner.

—James Douglas,
The Morning Leader.

Great poets are obscure for two opposite reasons; now, because they are talking about something too large for anyone to understand, and now, again, because they are talking about something too small for anyone to see. Francis Thompson possessed both these infinities.... He was describing the evening earth with its mist and fume and fragrance, and represented the whole as rolling upwards like a smoke; then suddenly he called the whole ball of the earth a thurible, and said that some gigantic spirit swung it slowly before God. This is the case of the image too large for comprehension; another instance sticks in my mind of the image which is too small. In one of his poems he says that the abyss between the known and the unknown is bridged by "Pontifical death." There are about ten historical and theological puns in that one word. That a priest means a pontiff, that a pontiff means a bridge-maker, that death is certainly a bridge, that death may turn out after all to be a reconciling priest, that at least priest and bridges both attest to the fact that one thing can get separated from another thing—these ideas, and twenty more, are all tacitly concentrated in the word "Pontifical." In Francis Thompson's poetry, as in the poetry of the universe, you can work infinitely out and out, but yet infinitely in and in. These two infinities are the mark of greatness; and he was a great poet.

—G. K. Chesterton,
The Illustrated London News.

Thompson used his large vocabulary with a boldness—and especially a recklessness, almost a frivolity in rhyme—that were worthy of Browning. On the other hand, these rugged points were, at a further view, absorbed into the total effect of beauty in a manner which Browning never achieved; for the poet, entirely

free from timidity in matters of poetic form, relied not on chastity
or perfection of detail, but on the perfervid rush of his genius,
which simply carried his readers over the rough places. Here was
a large utterance—large in bulk, in speed, in a lavish disregard
of economy, and yet, what could not for a moment be mistaken
was that the poetry was at once great and sincere. These *Sister
Songs*, written in praise of two little sisters, contain a number of
lovely and most musical lines, and some passages—such as the
seventh section of the first poem—which Spenser would not have
disowned.

—*The Times.*

The greater a poet's message, the more profound his thought,
the larger his range, and the more exquisite his note, the deeper
and more incessant will be his demand upon his reader. That
is why the great poets have had to wait for their recognition.
Only the few will or can co-operate at the beginning, but they
are the leaven; and now whole masses can see the poetic purport
of Shelley, Coleridge, Keats and Wordsworth, of whom the
contemporary criticism was a thing over which you laugh or cry,
as the mood has you. Those who see in Mr Francis Thompson an
authentic poet have at any rate the profound interest of watching
the various stages in the making of their immortal. How have
the portents followed the precedent afforded by the poets just
named? In general, very accurately, we think. The common
attitude of critics towards them and him has been very similar—
in the case of Shelley it is so near in its very wording as to be
sometimes startling. Extravagances and novelties of diction, a
toppling over of images, and "obscurity"—of course that—were
dwelt upon by objectors—very just objectors, no doubt—who
busied and troubled about details, lost all sense of proportion,
and had no ear for the great and ultimate meaning of the poet's
message.... The note that comes most majestically from Mr
Thompson is that of the reconciliation of the two natures and
destinies of man. To that literal oneness Wordsworth groped in

his merely "kindred points of heaven and home." Of that oneness Rossetti has the hint, and Coventry Patmore the full vision. Mr Thompson is the heir of the poets, and he has entered fully into his inheritance. He has not picked their flowers and worn them fading; their seed has passed into his life, and they have blossomed anew.

—*The Academy.*

No other among the younger poets so effectually proclaimed a mastery of the grand style: none other had so securely occupied a position on the right side of the line which for ever separates inspiration from talent, poetry from agreeable verse. He appeared on the scene fully equipped. There were no long years of public neglect, or production of volumes which lay unnoticed on the bookstalls before being cast into the dust heap. The marvellous splendour of his first volume revealed a writer of no common order; with a secureness of touch, a magical decoration of style, and a real message behind all the pomp and glitter and dazzling display. It was art not for art's sake, but charged with a meaning and a name. *The Hound of Heaven* was hailed by all competent critics as one of the great religious poems of this time or of any time.

—*The Daily News.*

FOOTNOTES:

[1] The umbrage of an elm-tree, described earlier
    in the Sister Songs from which this and the
    six succeeding poems are detached.
[2] The chant of the Mistress of Vision, whom, in her
    secret garden, the Poet has earlier described.
[3] The Earth.
[4] Who had passed before him in ghostly procession—the
    "holy poets," the soldiers, sailors, and men of science.
[5] Cloud-shapes often observed by travellers in the East.
[6] This Poem (found among his papers when he died) Francis
    Thompson might yet have worked upon to remove, here a
    defective rhyme, there an unexpected elision. But no altered
    mind would he have brought to its main purport; and the
    prevision of "Heaven in Earth and God in Man," pervading his
    earlier published verse, we find here accented by poignantly
    local and personal allusions. For in these triumphing
    stanzas, he held in retrospect those days and nights of
    human dereliction he spent beside London's River, and in
    the shadow—but all radiance to him—of Charing Cross.

Made in the USA
Monee, IL
11 November 2022

17437818R00111